The Shulamite's Cry

Discover Your Journey in The Song of Solomon

Beauty Realm
PUBLISHERS
KANSAS CITY, MO

Mike Brumback
foreword by Bob Sorge

The Shulamite's Cry

Copyright © 2009 by Mike Brumback
Revised December 2010
Beauty Realm Publishers
Kansas City, MO 64137
mikebrumback@ihop.org

This book or parts thereof may not be reproduced in any form, except for brief quotations in reviews, without written permission from the publisher. All rights reserved.

Unless otherwise noted, all Scripture quotations are from the *New King James Version of the Bible*. Copyright © 1979, 1980, 1982 by Thomas Nelson, Inc., publishers. Used by permission.

Scripture quotations marked NIV are from the *Holy Bible, New International Version*. Copyright © 1973, 1978, 1984, International Bible Society. Used by permission.

Scripture quotations are taken from the *Complete Jewish Bible*, Copyright © 1998 by David H. Stern. Published by Jewish New Testament Publications, Inc. Used by Permission.

Scripture quotations are taken from the GNB, *Good News Bible*, Copyright © 2000, 2001, 2002 by the American Bible Society. First Published by Good News for Modern Man in 1996. Used by Permission.

All Hebrew Word Definitions are taken from the Study Light Website–www.studylight.org and the *PC Study Bible*–version 2.1.

Cover design by Nance Coggeshall
Edited by Hollie Carney
Typesetting by Dale Jimmo

ISBN 9780981999708

Printed in the United States of America

Dedication

To all of God's wonderful people who have a difficult time understanding the Song of Solomon and struggle seeing themselves as the Bride of Christ, especially the men.

I gladly dedicate and devote this book to you and pray that you will have a divine encounter of the fiery love of Jesus, the Bridegroom God. I know this is your cry!

Contents

Introduction 1

1 Overview of The Song of Solomon 5

2 Your Cry for Intimacy 23

3 The King's Chambers 39

4 Facing Your Identity Crisis 53

5 Learning to be Still before Jesus 71

6 The Discipline of God 89

7 The Ravished Bridegroom God 111

8 The Fellowship of Sufferings 139

9 The Bridal Seal of Fire 171

Appendix 192

Other Products by Mike Brumback 193

Resources by Bob Sorge 195

Foreword

The longing for God is the universal cry of the human heart.

Many, however, have not been awakened to the true nature of their inner longing. Consequently, they seek to quench the thirst of their soul in ways that might temporarily dull their appetites but can never satisfy the great longings of the heart.

It is a happy day when the human heart is awakened to the pursuit of God. This kindness has been extended to you. You are reading this book because of your cry–"Jesus, I want You! I want to know You! I want to feel Your nearness. I have to know that our love is real. Jesus, bring me into mature intimacy with You!"

This is a prayer that the Lord loves to answer. In fact, He has given us the Scriptures as His gift to enable us to find our way into that relationship.

Perhaps one of the greatest portions of Scripture to empower our intimacy with God is the Song of Solomon. However, when you read the Song of Solomon for the first time, the power of its message will likely elude you. And that's why the book you hold in your hands is so helpful. Mike Brumback opens up the Song of Solomon in such clear, understandable ways that you are empowered to join the Shulamite in the book and make her journey your own.

If you'll let it, this book will open your understanding to the journey that each of us must take in coming into full bridal partnership with our Lord Jesus Christ. And in case the term "bridal partnership" seems overly-feminine to any of the men reading this book, I just want to point out that the Song of Solomon was written by a man's man. Furthermore, the masculine touch on Mike's pen reinforces the fact that intimacy with Jesus is as much the domain of the brothers as the sisters in Christ.

Read this book carefully and prayerfully, and as you read, draw near in your heart to God. If you do, I assure you that He will draw near to you!

Bob Sorge
Kansas City, Missouri
July 13, 2009

Introduction

If this book has found its way into your hands, then whether you realize it or not, the cry of your heart has reached the throne of God. The deep longings of your heart are about to usher you into your destiny as a mature bridal partner with the Lover of your soul. Your hidden cry to love Jesus has deeply moved His heart, and He is so excited to answer your cry. Simply said: you have been on a prophetic journey to come forth as a wholehearted lover of God, and you are about to discover that the secret cry of your heart has been the greatest weapon you have possessed to get you there.

So what is the Shulamite's cry all about? Who is the Shulamite? What does the Shulamite's cry have to do with you and I? I will address all three questions and explain.

First: Who is the Shulamite? She is the maiden in the Song of Solomon who becomes the Bride of Christ. She is a farm girl who worked in the vineyard and tended sheep. The Shulamite represents every sincere believer (male or female, young and old) who has a love and passion for Jesus Himself. As we look at the first four chapters of the Song of Solomon, I refer to her as the Shulamite. The reason is because she is not yet a mature Bride. She is immature, weak, easily distracted and selfish. She is more focused upon what she can receive out of her relationship with her Beloved. But she loves God very much and has a big cry in her heart to fully abandon herself to Him. Her cry and loving obedience is her greatness! In looking at the last four chapters of Song of Solomon, I refer to her as the Bride. The reason is because she is now mature in her love and is serving God for His ultimate pleasure and enjoyment. The relationship is more about what He can receive from it. She is fully His inheritance. She is the one who captures the eyes of her Beloved.

Second: What is the Shulamite's cry all about? It portrays the journey of the Shulamite in the Song of Solomon. She is constantly seeking after her Beloved and is being trained within her soul to become just like Him in every area of her life. She wants to shine like the stars in the universe (see Philippians 2:13-14).She has a deep longing to become Jesus' supreme possession and abide under His Lordship. She moves into a radical obedience and will be ushered into having the bridal seal of fire burning within her. It is her supreme cry. And it's Jesus' supreme cry as well.

> *Set me as a seal upon your heart, As a seal upon your arm; For love is as strong as death, Jealousy as cruel as the grave, Its flames are flames of fire, A most vehement flame. Many waters cannot quench love, Nor can the floods drown it. If a man would give for love All the wealth of his house, It would be utterly despised.*
> Song of Solomon 8:6–7

It is important to know that as the Shulamite is in pursuit of becoming a Bride, she has many deep struggles and issues arising within her own soul. She has come to grasp the constant tension of loving God; yet a battle rages deep inside. There are many areas that have to be conquered in her soul. But she is willing to face them head on with her Beloved. She is willing to go the distance for love. It is her sincere cry and willingness to obey that will help her all the way in her journey through the wilderness.

Third: What does the Shulamite's cry have to do with you and I? This is our journey and our story that we are discovering. The cry that we see in the heart of the Shulamite is the same cry that we yearn for. We are the Shulamites. We are on

Introduction

a pilgrimage, longing and yearning to experience the heart of the Bridegroom God, and become His private garden and inheritance. Just like the Shulamite, we all have many hidden struggles that war within, whether we admit it or not. We are weak and broken and stumble so many times. But we are chasing after the heart of God and His beautiful Kingdom. We won't give up or give in. We are destined for greatness! We have a big cry inside us to be restored and made whole in our emotions. We desire to be fully mature, both spiritually and emotionally. We long to fully abandon ourselves to God's will and purposes in our lives, no matter how difficult the struggle. Not only will we set our heart on living this type of lifestyle, but we will actually live it out in a personal and practical way. This is what the Shulamite's cry is all about.

Before I finish this introduction, let me explain in more detail about the power of a secret cry. The whole focus of this book peers into the hidden cry within the Shulamite's heart. It reveals her deepest longings to be dedicated to the Lord even before she walks it out in a mature way, although she will follow through with her commitment. Her cry to love and obey is a cry that nobody can see but God Himself. He sees. Her cry is that place deep inside her soul that keeps reaching out to God for help. It keeps reaching out to heaven, because she knows her own barrenness and poverty.

This is your journey. It is your destiny. It is the cry of your heart. You must believe how powerful you are on the inside, because of the big yes inside you. God sees your cry. Your cry to love God may seem insignificant to you, but it's not to Him. He wants to draw out your greatness. Your cry reveals what you set your heart upon. Your cry is how God defines you. It's what touches His heart more than anything else. Even your weakest cry catches the eyes of the Beloved. There is nothing more powerful than the power of your cry within the chambers of your heart. Be encouraged!

When the Scriptures talk about crying, it is not referring to outward tears, although that might be taking place;

it's referring to something that is going on deep inside the heart. Do you believe that there is a gold mine in your heart? Yes! It's your cry. Do you realize that your greatest weapon you possess is your cry? It's not your talent, gifting, reputation, leadership skills or wealth, but it's the hidden cry within. The power of the cry is found in its desperation. It is being desperate to encounter God's heart at a new level. It's being desperate to change from the old habits that hold you down. It's being desperate to feel cherished and embraced and not forsaken.

As we study the life of the Shulamite–who becomes the Bride in the Song of Solomon–we see how her cry to love Jesus is what sustained her through the journey of pain and difficulty. It was her cry that caused her to come up from the wilderness with a leaning heart.

> *Who is this coming up from the wilderness, leaning upon her beloved?*
> Song of Solomon 8:5

I want to invite you on a journey with me as we allow the Holy Spirit to birth and produce a deeper cry to love Jesus and to become just like Him within the garden of our heart. Let us become champions on the inside and have a big cry for our Beloved. Let us act upon the hidden cry that's inside us. May we say yes to Shulamite's cry as we travel through the Song of all Songs–the Song of Solomon.

CHAPTER ONE
Overview of Song of Solomon

I remember the first time I read the Song of Solomon it seemed very strange and definitely too romantic for me, especially as a male. There was so much confusion racing through my mind. The intensity of the language made me feel uncomfortable. I was reading about kisses, chambers, gardens, lilies, cheeks, lovesickness, turtledoves, gazelles, hair like a flock of goats, fragrances and so on. I purposely would skip this book when reading the Bible. I basically never gave it a chance to speak for itself! But over the last ten years, to my surprise, the Song of Solomon has become one of my favorite books in Scripture. It did not come so easy or so fast. It took time to understand the language and journey of the Shulamite. And it took time to embrace the call upon my life as the Bride of Christ. That was probably the most difficult thing for me. I thought the revelation of the Bride was only for women and not for men. I was fearful that the Song of Solomon would undermine my masculinity. But just the opposite has happened; it has strengthened my manhood and released me to fully accept who God the Father created me to be–a Bride, ruling and reigning with Jesus, the Bridegroom God.

To be the Bride has nothing to do with gender. It doesn't mean we have to imagine a woman wearing a wedding dress to be the Bride of Christ, especially for us men. But it means, as men and women, young and old, we have been called into a deep, intimate friendship with the God of all beauty. Not even the angels have access into the interior of God's radiant emotions, but we do. What I really love about the Song of Solomon is how it teaches us to grow into becoming a mature Bride. I don't mean theologically, but emotionally. Growing into and becoming the Bride of Christ is our future destiny!

> *Then one of the seven angels who had the seven bowls filled with the seven last plagues came to me and talked with me, saying, "Come," I will show you the bride, the Lamb's wife.*
>
> Revelation 21:9

To Be the Bride Reveals Three Distinct Realities

1. It's a position of nearness and privilege to the heart of Jesus. It's called *intimacy*.
2. It's about growing into bridal maturity and character with Jesus, the Beloved. It's called *maturity*.
3. It's about submitting and living under Jesus' Lordship. We are His inheritance. It's called *submission*.

The first reality of being the Bride is our fuel and motivation to everything we do. It is where we discover Jesus' burning passion for us and feel close to Him in intimacy. The second reality of being the Bride is the place where we learn to grow up emotionally. It's not enough to be spiritually mature in gifting and in leadership, but we must be mature in how we relate to God Himself and how we relate to others in relationships. The third reality of being the Bride is where our rights, demands, desires, reputation, time and money are fully surrendered under Jesus' leadership. It's called absolute submission to God's desires and purposes. That's the great mark of bridal maturity!

We can see a progression of these three realities in the story line of the Shulamite. She begins with intimacy in chapters 1 and 2; then she's learning to grow into maturity in chapters 3–5, and then she moves into submitting her life and control under Jesus' Lordship in chapters 6–8.

Here are a few Bible passages that you can study to help you to better understand the revelation of the Bride of Christ.

Daughters of kings are among your honored women; at your right hand is the royal bride in gold of Ophir.
Psalm 45:9, NIV

For as a young man marries a virgin, so shall your sons marry you; and as the bridegroom rejoices over the bride, so shall your God rejoice over you.
Isaiah 62:5

Then I will cause to cease from the cities of Judah and from the streets of Jerusalem the voice of mirth and the voice of gladness, the voice of the bridegroom and the voice of the bride. For the land shall be desolate.
Jeremiah 7:34

He who has the bride is the bridegroom; but the friend of the bridegroom, who stands and hears him, rejoices greatly because of the bridegroom's voice. Therefore this joy of mine is fulfilled.
John 3:29

Then I, John, saw the holy city, New Jerusalem, coming down out of heaven from God, prepared as a bride adorned for her husband.
Revelation 21:2

And the Spirit and the bride say, "Come!" And let him who hears say, "Come!" And let him who thirsts come. Whoever desires, let him take the water of life freely.
Revelation 22:17

Until we understand why Jesus shed His own precious blood and died at Calvary, we will have a difficult time understanding the depths of the Song of Solomon. Why did Jesus die? It is because He wanted to marry us forever, ruling and reigning with Him in bridal partnership. He is a God who has burning passion and great delight over those who love Him in secret. Jesus is a Husband and He longs for a bridal partner, a wife. He came to betroth us to Himself. He has betrothed us in five distinct ways: in righteousness, justice, lovingkindness, mercy and faithfulness.

> *I will betroth you to Me forever; Yes, I will betroth you to Me In **righteousness** and **justice**, In **lovingkindness** and **mercy**; I will betroth you to Me in **faithfulness**, And you shall know the Lord.*
> Hosea 2:19–20, emphasis added

The Song of Solomon is a book of holy romance and holy fire. John Wesley describes the Song of Solomon as a book that breathes forth the hottest flames of love between Christ and His people. God is raising up a generation of believers who will go deep in this glorious book and proclaim it to the nations of the earth. The Holy Spirit is going to answer the meaning and purpose of life in this love song, and will usher a generation into wholehearted love with the Bridegroom God.

If you feel like maybe this book is not for you, then just look at these great preachers in history, who have given themselves to it. The Song of Solomon was a favorite book of D.L. Moody, C.H. Spurgeon and St. John of the Cross. John Gill, a Puritan preacher, developed 122 sermons from it; Bernard of Clairvaux, a French mystic, brought forth 86 teachings from chapter one alone.

Some say that the Song of Solomon is not quoted in the New Testament, yet there are fragments everywhere:
- A well of living waters (see John 4)
- The veiled woman (see 1 Corinthians 11)
- The fig tree (see Luke 21:29)
- Myrrh and fragrant oils (see John 19)
- The spotless bride (see Ephesians 5)

- Unquenchable love (see 1 Corinthians 13)
- Love strong as death (see John 15)
- Ointment poured forth (see John 12)
- Draw me (see John 6)
- The Shepherd leading His flock (see John 10)
- The beautiful King (see Revelation 19)

It is my prayer that you open your heart to get a vision of the Song of Solomon and your eternal destiny, to shine forth as a radiant and glorious Bride (see Revelation 19:7–8). I want to encourage you to go and get your Bible and open to the Song of Solomon right now. I personally recommend the New King James version for the Song of Solomon. It's the translation that I am using. It is important for you to become familiar with the language and the characters in this glorious love song. Whenever I give any Scripture references, I encourage you to turn to them and ask the Holy Spirit to write them deeply in the scroll of your heart. Does that sound good?

Overview of Song of Solomon

The Song of Solomon was written in approximately 900–950, B.C. by Solomon, King David's son. We are told that he was the wisest king ever, besides Jesus Himself. Solomon wrote 1,005 songs and uttered 3,000 proverbs (see 1 Kings 4:29–34). He was a great songwriter. He probably wrote the Song of Solomon before his spiritual decline (see 1 Kings 11:3–4). Of all the songs he wrote, this is the best and most precious one. It is one of the greatest love songs of all ages. This book is actually not a story; it is a song–"The Song of all Songs." The Hebrew word for "song" in Song of Solomon 1:1 is *shiyr*. It means musical singing; a lyric song or a song of levitical choirs.

This song is what awakens holy romance and lovesickness within the heart. It reveals how we grow in passion for

Jesus. Every chapter roars with the beauty of Jesus' affections and emotions, and reveals the Bride's spiritual identity. Within the Song of Songs lies the heartbeat of Jesus Christ and His yearning to bring forth a bridal partner to share His throne.

> *To him who overcomes I will grant to sit with Me on My throne, as I also overcame and sat down with My Father on His throne.*
>
> Revelation 3:21

The Song of Solomon is an unbroken love song that continues for over eight chapters that empowers and equips the human heart for the journey of the end–times (see Song of Solomon 8:5). The eight chapters reveals eight distinct seasons in the Shulamite's life. Maybe you're asking the question: how does the Song of Solomon equip the human heart? How will it affect my heart for the coming difficulty? I believe it's by the constant affirmation of Jesus over the hearts of His Shulamites. He is the One who will tell you how lovely you are, even in your deepest struggle. As we study the life of the Shulamite, we will discover that Jesus never once says anything negative about her, but He only speaks positively over her, and calls her forth to who she will become in His eyes. He prophetically keeps telling her over and over how beautiful she is. Simply said: the very best cheerleader the Shulamite has on her journey is God Himself!

What is so wonderful about this prophetic song from heaven is the exchange of declarations of love between Jesus, the Bridegroom, and the Shulamite, who becomes the Bride. They both are constantly boasting of each other and praising each other's beauty. It is an overflow of two lovers who just can't keep silent about each other. Every time they open their mouth to speak, it just flows like a river. Their entire conversation is about one main thing: how beautiful and how great they are in each other's eyes. It's the song and praise of divine love!

Overview of Song of Solomon

The setting of the drama in this book is Jerusalem. The gospel of Matthew calls Jerusalem "the city of the great King." The prophets spoke of Israel as the wife of Jehovah. Hosea, especially, dwelt on that theme. Jerusalem is the place the Father has chosen for His Beloved Son to rule and reign forever. The Lamb of God is destined to be crowned King in Jerusalem (see Jeremiah 3:17). He will be seen as beautiful and glorious during the 1,000-year Millennial reign. He will take His leadership and instruct the nations of the earth in righteousness. It's not going to be a work of man, but the very work of God–through the life and leadership of the Jewish Man from Nazareth. It is the Father who has appointed His Son to be the head and has given Him all authority!

> *And He put all things under His feet, and gave Him to be head over all things to the church, which is His body, the fullness of Him who fills all in all.*
> Ephesians 1:22–23

The Song of Solomon is a small poetic book of only one hundred and seventeen verses tucked away in the Old Testament, between Ecclesiastes and Isaiah, and is easily overlooked. It is one of the most neglected and misunderstood books in the Bible, and the reader who is going through the Word of God for the first time is usually puzzled when he comes to it. It is a book that has been greatly abused by people who have not understood it.

We do not have to be confused or frustrated when we read the Song of Solomon. It is a wonderful book that can ignite a flame in your heart. If you love poetry, then you should find yourself being swept up into a river of pleasure. But even if you don't enjoy poetry, you can still find this book to be very valuable to your own soul. This song is highly explosive in the arena of love.

There are five poetic books in the Bible: Job, Psalms, Proverbs, Ecclesiastes and the Song of Solomon. Each of these books teaches us valuable lessons about our God and how we relate to Him. Job is the voice of the Holy Spirit, revealing the fairness and beauty of God's heart as He allows pain and suffering in the lives of His godly ones. Everything He does is right and perfect. Psalms is a book of the heart, and it reflects every emotion known to man. It teaches you how to find encouragement in your deepest struggle. The book of Proverbs is the expression of the will of man, telling you how to live wisely. It highlights the power of wisdom and understanding. The book of Ecclesiastes is the voice of the mind of man. It is man searching for meaning and satisfaction apart from God Himself. The Song of Solomon is a powerful book that has a unique way of grabbing hold of the heart, giving revelation of Jesus' heart and desire for His beloved Bride. He has a 'cherishing heart' and a 'ravished heart' over the life of the Shulamite.

Two Main Interpretations

There are two main interpretations of the Song of Solomon. The first one is the "natural interpretation," which depicts a literal human love story between King Solomon and the Shulamite. It is a story based on biblical principles written to honor and inspire deeper love and intimacy within marriage. The natural interpretation has become very popular in the last hundred years.

The second interpretation is the "allegorical interpretation," depicting a story that is symbolic. This interpretation illustrates truths that are solidly revealed in the Word of God, making them easy to understand, just as Christ Jesus many times taught His disciples through parables. The allegorical interpretation has been the most common interpretation for the last 1,900 years of church history. There are three different allegorical interpretations that are used.

First: It's the relationship between God as the Bridegroom, and ethnic Israel as His Bride (see Jeremiah 2:2; Hosea 2:16–20; Ezekiel 16:8–38; Isaiah 54:5–6). This was the primary approach of the scribes in Old Testament times, as well as Jewish rabbis today.

Second: It's the relationship between Jesus and the corporate Church throughout history.

Third: It's the relationship between Jesus and the individual believer. This approach gives spiritual principles that help us in our passion for Jesus. This will be the approach that I will take in this study of the Song of Solomon.

Main Characters of the Book

King Solomon spiritually represents Jesus, the Bridegroom God. He is the glory of the entire book. It is inconceivable for the Holy Spirit to inspire a book in the Bible without Jesus being the predominant theme and center of attention. The Holy Spirit has a deep, intimate friendship with Jesus, and He is determined to make His beauty known to all the nations.

Here are some natural facts about Solomon:

- The Hebrew word for Solomon is *Shelomoh*. It means peace.

- Solomon is mentioned four times in the Song (3:9, 11; 8:11, 12). His name is also associated with the tents and curtains of chapter 1.

- Solomon was a very wealthy person. He had a country estate on the slopes of Mount Hermon. He used it as a retreat from pressures of being king in Jerusalem.

- Solomon is pictured with the crown upon His head in chapter 3. This is the glorious reality of Jesus, the slain King, being crowned by the Church.

Go forth, O daughters of Zion, and see King Solomon with the crown with which his mother crowned him on the day of his wedding, the day of the gladness of

his heart.
Song of Solomon 3:11

The Shulamite woman is the maiden who becomes the Bride of Christ. She is mentioned twice by name (6:13). She lived in Shunam (north of Jezreel). She is a farm girl who worked in the vineyard and tended sheep. The place where she worked was along a caravan route there in the hill country. Her own family were tenant farmers on one of the vineyards owned by Solomon. She starts out very immature, but becomes mature in love and in righteousness at the end of her journey. She is the one who captures the eyes of her Beloved!

- The Hebrew word for Shulamite is *Shuwlammiyth*. It means "the perfect" or "the peaceful."
- She is being perfected into a bridal partner for Jesus Himself.

Before I was even aware, My soul had make me As the chariots of my noble people.
Song of Solomon 6:12

The Daughters of Jerusalem are a group of believers who never attain the same degree of intimacy and maturity as the Bride. They don't have the same dedication and hunger as she does. They serve God at a distance. They are spending more time watching the Shulamite and asking her questions than just simply loving and obeying the Lord. But there are two times in the Song where they are being touched in a deep and personal way. In chapter 3, they are seen paving the interior of the wedding chariot with love. And in chapter 6, they want to seek after the Beloved with the Bride. I think it's important to give credit where it is due.

He made its pillars of silver, its support of gold, its seat of purple, its interior paved with love by the daughters of Jerusalem.
Song of Solomon 3:10

Overview of Song of Solomon

Where has your beloved gone, O fairest among women? Where has your beloved turned aside, that we may seek him with you?

Song of Solomon 6:1

- The Hebrew word for Daughters is *Bath*. It means young women. The Hebrew word for Jerusalem is *Yeruwshalaim*. It means the chief city of Palestine and the capital of the united kingdom of Israel and the kingdom of Judah after the split.
- The Daughters of Jerusalem are mentioned ten times in the Song (1:5; 2:2, 7; 3:5, 10, 11; 5:8, 16; 6:9; 8:4).

The watchmen were those who stood on watch towers (see Isaiah 21:5) and on walls of cities (see Isaiah 62:6). They kept the peace and raised the cry of alarm when necessary. They represent the spiritual leaders in the body of Christ who watched over the condition of men's souls and exercised spiritual authority. They are mentioned in Song of Solomon 3:3 and 5:7. The Hebrew word for watchmen is Shamar. It means to keep guard, observe, give help, protect and to watch over. They were guardsmen. They all had different stations of duty:

- In streets of cities (see Psalm 127:1)
- In Babylon (see Jeremiah 51:12)
- Around the Temple in Jerusalem on special occasions (see 2 Kings 11:6)

I believe there are two types of watchmen in the Song of Solomon. The watchmen in Song of Solomon 3 are leaders who help the Shulamite reach her highest destiny in God. I call them the "David watchmen." The reason is because their heart and leadership are like David's. They call you forth in your weakness and never condemn you. They are not threatened or intimidated by your spiritual progress. They will do anything to help you grow into mature love and

Christ–likeness. They are after God's own heart. The David watchmen have two distinct qualities about them:

1. They motivate you to be a person after God's own heart. We see this in the life of David in Psalm 27:4. He had one desire in life and that was to behold and discover the beauty of God's heart. The revelation of God's beauty is what produces a heart to chase after God's heart.

2. They have a strong desire to help others in their journey with God. We see this in David's life in 1 Samuel 20. Jonathan, who was King Saul's son, reveals his loyalty to David. Then David declares to Jonathan how he was the one who helped bring him into a Covenant with God and with himself. David definitely helped Jonathan in his walk with God (see 1 Samuel 20:8).

The watchmen in Song of Solomon 5 are leaders who are very jealous and threatened by the Bride, as she is growing into spiritual maturity. I call them the "Saul watchmen" because their heart and leadership are like Saul's. They are after their own reputation and interest. They will do anything, including spiritual abuse, in order to stop or hinder the Bride's journey in God. They have an agenda to use her for their own sakes and will throw spears at any cost. We can definitely see this in the life of Saul, who wanted to kill David (see 1 Samuel 19:9–10).

Two Main Sections of the Book

First: Chapters 1–4 focus on the Shulamite. She is immature and is mostly serving God on her terms. Yes, she is a lover of God and has a big cry to grow deeper in maturity, but she's more concerned about what she can receive out of the relationship with her Beloved. It is mostly about her receiving her inheritance in God.

Second: Chapters 5–8 focus on the Shulamite as a Bride.

Overview of Song of Solomon

She is now mature and is serving God on His terms. She is submitting under His Lordship. She is not perfect, but loves Jesus for His ultimate pleasure. It is all about Jesus receiving His reward and inheritance in the Bride.

The Progression of the Song

The journey begins with the Shulamite's cry for intimacy (1:2) and ends with her heart being sealed with the bridal seal, the very flame of the Bridegroom's love (8:6–7). She begins in the King's chambers (1:4) and under the apple tree (2:3), feasting on the beauty of her God. She then is beckoned by her Beloved to go up to the mountains with Him (2:10–14), but she refuses and is disciplined for it (3:1). She ends up out in the streets of Jerusalem, searching for her Beloved.

The focus of the book completely shifts in the middle, when she says yes to go to the mountains and leave her comfort zone. Let's read this wonderful verse that begins to change and transform the Shulamite into a Bride.

> *Until the day breaks and the shadows flee away, I will go my way to the mountain of myrrh and to the hill of frankincense.*
>
> Song of Solomon 4:6

She is now willing to go her way to the mountain of myrrh. After she says yes, she goes through the most difficult test on her journey. It is the dark night of her soul (5:2–7). However, once she passes through her time in the wilderness and is willing to obey her Beloved at all costs, she then receives a stunning revelation of her beauty from Him. He boldly praises her before His Father and all the hosts of heaven (6:4–10). She is now a bridal partner with her Beloved. She is pictured as doing everything together with Him (7:10–12). At the end of her prophetic journey, she becomes a mature Bride, sealed with the fire of the Bridegrooms love.

She is completely His inheritance (8:5–7).

The story line of the Shulamite describes the inevitable seasons in every single believer's life on the journey to wholehearted love. I believe we go through many of these seasons several times, at different levels and with different variations each time. Knowing and understanding the seasons in our life brings an incredible comfort and strength to our hearts. The purpose of the difficult seasons is to fully become Jesus' inheritance and submit under His Lordship, as the Father has promised His Son a gift on His wedding day. It's not about our happiness or what we can receive from this relationship, but it's about His happiness and what He can receive from this relationship. It is about Jesus receiving His inheritance for His wedding day, "the day of the gladness of His heart."

> *Go forth, O Daughters of Zion, And see King Solomon with the crown With which his mother crowned him On the day of his wedding, The day of the gladness of his heart.*
>
> Song of Solomon 3:11

Cultivating a Devotional Life Using the Song of Solomon

The language of the Song of Solomon might begin awkwardly, but in time, the simple phrases will become one of the most valuable possessions owned by your soul. However, this Song will not help you very much if the language of it does not get into your personal prayer life with your Beloved. Only learning concepts with your mind will not change your emotions or transform the garden of your heart. This love song must be turned into an active and prayerful dialogue with God's heart in order for it to come alive in you. You must read it in a devotional way, as though it were a duet sung by you and the Lord Jesus, right there in your living room. These words of love will fill your heart to live abandoned unto your

Overview of Song of Solomon

Lover as you pray different passages that touch your heart. You will find your relationship growing when you learn to talk directly to God Himself.

There is a *progression of revelation* that takes place in our lives when we take the truths of what the Scriptures say, and turn it into a personal dialogue with God's heart. Let me just give you an idea of what should be taking place as we are pursuing the Lord in the Song of Solomon.

- Academic Study
- Meditation
- Praying Bible Passages
- Singing the Word of God

We begin with academic study! This is the time when you read the Song of Solomon and begin to study different commentaries on it. You might pull out a Strong's concordance or dictionary. It is the time when you are gathering all the information and framing an overview of the book. It's a time mostly spent regarding information.

Then we have the time of meditation! This is when you take all the gathered information on the Song of Solomon and begin to meditate on it in your mind. To meditate means to ponder and go over and over what is being said. There are many benefits to mediation (see Psalm 1:2–3).

Then we have the time of praying the Bible passages! This is when you take the information and your time of meditation and you begin to get the bridal language of the Song into your prayer life. You actually pray the truths of who Jesus, the Bridegroom God is and you pray the truths of who you are to Him. There is nothing in your entire life that will ever surpass the impact of doing this. I'm serious!

I recommend praying aloud when you pray through the Song of Solomon, because when you speak the truths of what God says about you, your faith begins to grow. When you speak out loud you can hear yourself speaking. Doesn't faith come by hearing? So for instance, when you say to God that you are His beloved, as in Song of Solomon 6:3, and you hear yourself say it, eventually you will be convinced of it. It definitely works. You must realize how powerful your voice is to the Lord. In fact, He is the one who says in Song of Solomon 2, that He loves to hear your voice.

> *O my dove, in the clefts of the rock, in the secret places of the cliff, let me see your face, **let me hear your voice**; for your voice is sweet, and your face is lovely.*
> Song of Solomon 2:14, emphasis added

Finally, we have singing the Word of God! This is the most important and the most critical. It is when you take the information of the Word and turn it into a time of singing. Paul the Apostle tells us to sing with our spirit and sing with our understanding.

> *What is the conclusion then? I will pray with the spirit, and I will also pray with the understanding. I will sing with the spirit, and I will also sing with the understanding.*
> 1 Corinthians 14:15

Singing both the Word of God with our understanding and in the spirit (in heavenly language) is one of the most effective ways of taking the information in our minds and receiving it into our hearts. When we read and meditate upon Scripture, we mostly use our mind. But when we sing the Word of God and make a melody in our heart to God, we use our spirit. It's the key to go from head knowledge to heart knowledge. I not only sing to God's through the Word of God, but I also sing from God's heart to my heart, using my name and making it more personal. Here is the difference: When I sing to God, I say, God, I am your beloved. When I sing from God's heart to myself, I say, Michael, you are my beloved. It's a big difference. Singing the Scriptures out loud from God's heart to our heart is the key to a transformed life!

Overview of Song of Solomon

I remember the first time I tried this I felt so awkward and foolish. I thought I had to be a worship leader or singer to sing back Scripture to God's heart. But that is not true. After spending some time praying and singing the Word of God out loud, it has taken the passages from my mind into my heart. I cannot imagine living life without doing this. If you struggle to sing the Word of God out loud, then I encourage you to try offering silent whispers to God in your heart. The silent whispers inside the secret place of your heart will help cultivate your bridal love for Jesus. Here is a wonderful verse that I have briefly mentioned to whisper to Jesus in Song of Solomon 7.

> *I am my beloved's, and his desire is toward me.*
> Song of Solomon 7:10

It only takes a few seconds to do this. The silent whispers are very powerful! You can be in the midst of a crowd and can be communing in your spirit with the Bridegroom God. You can say to Him, "I am Yours and You are mine." Keep saying it until you begin to feel a little bit of what you are saying. God wrote on paper how He feels about you, so you must write it into your heart in order to feel what He feels.

Whispering silently and singing passages in the Song of Solomon are two excellent ways to set our hearts on fire. It will dismantle the lies and accusations the enemy tries to plant in our thought life. He always accuses the nature and character of God's heart and our spiritual identity. So we must sing back the Word of God and come into agreement with what God says about Himself and what He says about us as His Bride. Every time we do this we are shattering demonic strongholds in our minds and planting the truth into our spirits (see Colossians 3:16). It's called the power of agreement!

Let us begin right now to practice singing God's affection

over us and practice the silent whispers in our heart. Keep in mind as you sing a key passage from the Song of Solomon, the Holy Spirit will bring other Scriptures to your mind that relate to that passage. That's where meditation comes in. It's like a bank account that you can draw from. As we do this on a regular basis, we will see a radical change within our lives: information to revelation, revelation to transformation, and transformation to impartation. Hallelujah!

Your Journey Into the Song of Solomon

This is your journey and your story that you are discovering. It's the cry of your heart! It is what is going to change your life forever. May you cry out for Jesus to mark and seal your heart from heaven with the kiss of His prophetic song. Would you ask the Holy Spirit to help you and teach you how to make the Song of Solomon a natural part of your secret prayer life? May you go after it with all of your heart and all of your strength. Be the generation who will be radically touched with unhindered revelation as you study, meditate, pray, sing and whisper the truths of this glorious love song–"the song of all songs."

CHAPTER TWO

Your Cry for Intimacy

Let him kiss me with the kisses of his mouth—For your love is better than wine.
Song of Solomon 1:2

The very first cry that comes from the heart of the Shulamite is her cry for the kiss of Jesus. She asked for the kisses of His mouth. The Hebrew word for "kiss" is *nashaq.* It is a token of friendly, affectionate union of hearts. It means to put together, to touch gently, to be around and to equip with weapons. This is exactly what is happening to her, she is being equipped with the weapon of love. She is entering into an affectionate union with God's heart. She wants Jesus to sing His affections over her. She longs to hear Him sing the song of His love into her heart. She wants her cold heart to be awakened and empowered with the kisses of revelation—the kiss of who He is. This is her first recorded prayer in the Song of Solomon.

When the Shulamite asks Jesus to kiss her with the kisses of His mouth, she is not referring to literal kisses that would imply sensuality. The kisses are a metaphor for intimacy with God. She understands that nobody can fill the void in her heart but Jesus Himself. He alone is her source and provision. He is the One who desires to reveal Himself to her. So how does He do this? It is through the Word of God that He reveals what He is like to her. The Word of God is the kiss that proceeds from His mouth.

> *...that He might make you know that man shall not live by bread alone; but man lives by every word that proceeds from the mouth of the Lord.*
>
> Deuteronomy 8:3

The Power of God's Word

It is the glory and power of the Word of God that can change and transform the human heart. Jesus Himself is the Word; His name is called the Word of God.

> *He is dressed in a robe dipped in blood, and his name is the Word of God.*
>
> Revelation 19:13

The theme of the Shulamite is her cry for the kisses of God's Word to touch the deepest and most broken places in her heart. She does not want to go on her journey without having her heart touched and inspired by the revelation of the Word of God. It is why she not only asked for a kiss, but she asked for many kisses. It's through the hunger of eating the Scroll from heaven that her heart will be sustained (see Colossians 3:16).

Just as the Shulamite cried out for the kisses of God's mouth, so we must cry out as well. We must realize that we will never grow in our spiritual journey without having fresh revelation from Jesus Himself–the Word of God. It is God's Word that transforms us as we understand the way God thinks and feels about us, especially in our brokenness. Jesus wants our hearts to come alive again! But there are no shortcuts to having a heart set on fire. We must have a vision to go deep in the Word of God and be utterly exhilarated. We must set a high priority to study the emotions of God's heart revealed in the Scriptures. It is how we are transformed into His likeness.

> *But we all, with unveiled face, beholding as in a mirror*

> *the glory of the Lord, are being transformed into the same image from glory to glory, just as by the Spirit of the Lord.*
>
> 2 Corinthians 3:18

> *And do not be conformed to this world, but be transformed by the renewing of your mind, that you may prove what is that good and acceptable and perfect will of God.*
>
> Romans 12:2

The Word of God is like a well that never runs dry. It's a personal love letter to us. It was written in the Father's heart before the foundations of the earth and revealed in His Beloved Son, Jesus! The Word of God is the only thing that will anchor our soul in truth and in righteousness. It is our road map on our journey to Zion. The Word of God is the divine kiss to a lost and dying generation!

So what is the primary purpose for the Shulamite to ask Jesus to come and kiss her heart with the kisses of His mouth? That's the question we need to be asking. It is because His love is better than wine. The Hebrew word for "better" in Song of Solomon 1:2 is *towb*. It means pleasant, more delightful, good, agreeable, rich, glad, joyful and happy. She knew that His love was more pleasant and joyful than anything she would ever experience in her life. The Sons of Korah used the same word "better" in Psalm 84 as was one of the themes in their song, related to the house of the Lord.

> *For a day in Your courts is better than a thousand. I would rather be a doorkeeper in the house of my God than dwell in the tents of wickedness.*
>
> Psalm 84:10

The secret to receiving the kiss of God's mouth is desiring the love of God. His love is better than anything, and it is what the Shulamite was craving the most. She simply wanted to be loved by God. It's that simple! Her cry was to be loved. That's the deepest cry of every human heart. She could not afford to have her heart grow cold on the inside. She was not content to just have a normal relationship with her Beloved, but she wanted something that would revolutionize her own heart and soul. She longed to feel cherished in her heart. She longed to encounter the pleasure of Jesus' passionate love. That is where she wanted to abide.

The Love of God

The love of God is what you and I are craving for, just like the Shulamite. It is the deep cry of our heart and souls. We are destined to be consumed by a love from another age. The love of Jesus, the Bridegroom God, is more satisfying than anything else in the world. There is nothing that compares to it.

The love of God is such a vast and supreme subject. It is the greatest attribute in God's heart. It's what the Old and New Covenants highlights the most. The love of God is the most powerful reality on the earth and is more exhilarating than the wine of this world. It is so pure, so fervent, and so intimate. This love in God's heart passes all knowledge.

> *That He would grant you, according to the riches of His glory, to be strengthened with might through His Spirit in the inner man, that Christ may dwell in your hearts through faith; that you, being rooted and grounded in love, may be able to comprehend with all the saints what is the width and length and depth and height– to know the love of Christ which passes knowledge; that you may be filled with all the fullness of God.*
> Ephesians 3:16–19

You and I were created for love and anything less will leave us starving for more. We will never be disappointed or

Your Cry For Intimacy 27

let down by the flame of love that is in the heart of the Bridegroom God. He longs and desires to ignite a flame within our hearts as we cry out to Him for it. One of our greatest weaknesses is our inability to know and admit how needy we really are. We must realize that it takes humility to be loved so profoundly and intensely. It requires the submissive posture of a Bride to receive God's pleasure in us. Until we have an encounter with Jesus' unconditional love, acceptance and affection in areas of our hidden core pain, it will be difficult to pour out love to others. We cannot love others until we first love ourselves, and we cannot love ourselves until we are convinced that God really loves us. This was the revelation given to John the Apostle. John tells us in his first epistle that it is God who first loved us. We cannot love God any more without first receiving His love for us. Jesus didn't wait to be loved; He took the first step to love. That's the mark of a great leader! When God wants to empower us to love Him, He first reveals Himself as One who loves.

We love Him because He first loved us.
                                                    1 John 4:19

When I talk about the love of God, I am talking about His affections and how He feels on the inside of His heart. He is a God who has deep feelings and intense passion for His Shulamites. It's our destiny to feel the outrageous love of God inside us.

I have heard at least a few hundred times that Jesus loved me and I did believe it, but I never felt that He *liked* me. Something very powerful took place in my heart when I felt just a little bit of how God felt for me. He was convincing me that He really liked me and that I was His favorite one, just as you also are His favorite one. I actually believed that He liked hanging out with me and that I was not a burden to Him. I felt wanted, pursued, desired and sensed that He was really interested in me. I felt that I was not the one that He was frustrated with, but was the one He enjoyed. It is the greatest feeling to experience. When this revelation touched my spirit, it was the kiss of God at its best. It helped set my heart on a journey to being a lover of God's heart. This would become my life vision and destiny upon the earth.

I don't believe we have a problem believing that God is love, but our struggle is believing that God is a lover. Do we understand what the New Testament teaches? The same way that God the Father loves His own Son is the same way that Jesus loves us. Yes, I mean the same way. How much does the Father love His Beloved Son? How does He feel about Him all the time? What does He think about when He ponders who He is? Your answer to these questions will open up a well that will mark your life forever.

As the Father loved Me, I also have loved you; abide in My love.

John 15:9

Jesus loving us as His Father loves Him is the kiss of His mouth, the kiss of His Word. What makes His love so unique is that it's unconditional. Unconditional love is never based on the performance of the person who is receiving it. It is based on the nature of the one giving it.

The love of God is what will sustain us in the darkest times. It's what will give us courage to face the most intense trials in life. If we have nothing to die for, we have nothing to live for. We must have a high vision of God's loving commitment for us that will be the anchor in our souls, especially when we face difficult times. In Revelation 15, we see the end–time martyrs standing upon the sea of glass, victorious in love. They are singing two great songs before the throne of God. They are singing the Song of Moses and the Song of the Lamb.

They sing the song of Moses, the servant of God, and the song of the Lamb, saying: "Great and marvelous are Your works, Lord God Almighty! Just and true are

> *Your ways, O King of the saints! Who shall not fear You, O Lord, and glorify Your name? For You alone are holy. For all nations shall come and worship before You, For Your judgments have been manifested."*
>
> Revelation 15:3–4

When we experience the Bridegroom's love in a very personal way, it is the greatest motivation for obedience. It will motivate us to live a life without complaining or arguing, causing us to shine like stars in the universe!

It will help us come into agreement with God's leadership over our lives, even if we don't fully understand what God is doing with us. Obedience to God is our love for Him (see John 14:15). There are three types of heart responses of obedience in Scripture. We definitely want the third one.

1. Disobedience
2. Mandatory Obedience
3. Voluntary Obedience

Voluntary obedience is where we go from duty to delight, from boredom to fascination, from a worker to a lover, from trying harder to enjoying more. We go from I must to I desire. We go from doing to receiving.

I believe so much of the body of Christ is living in mandatory obedience. They are serving God because they have to and not because they want to. The only solution to move us out of mandatory obedience and into voluntary obedience is a divine encounter with Jesus' unfailing and amazing love in a personal way. The Gospel is a call to live in the vast ocean of divine love. God's unconditional love dwells in us, and we want that seed of love to grow daily in the garden of our heart. When we begin to see how beautiful Jesus is and how He feels about us in our struggle, then we will begin to be ushered into voluntary obedience. Voluntary love is what moves God's heart more than anything else, and it's what will be our great reward in the age to come. Jesus will tell our story of how much we loved Him before His Father and all the hosts of angels.

> *He who overcomes shall be clothed in white garments, and I will not blot out his name from the Book of Life; but I will confess his name before My Father and before his angels.*
>
> Revelation 3:5

Remember, just as the Shulamite cried out in 1:2 for the kisses of Jesus' love, which is better than wine, so we must cry out also. It must be a prayer that consumes us. It must be something that provokes us and causes us to contend for the very fullness of God's heart. God's love is not passive, and we cannot be passive to receive it. Why don't you take a few minutes right now and begin crying out to Jesus, to receive His love, which is better than wine. Please don't move forward in reading this book until you have done it, even its only a few minutes, it really counts.

The Power of Intimacy

I believe the divine kiss of Jesus' mouth is the doorway into a life of intimacy. There is no greater calling on the earth than the calling of intimacy. It is what God Himself created us for. It is what separates Christianity from all other religions—a love relationship with the heart of God. It is the primary message of the Song of Solomon.

There are three metaphors of intimacy with God in the Song: the divine kiss (1:2), the divine embrace (2:5), and the divine seal (8:6). Intimacy with God is the easiest yet most difficult reality we will ever encounter. Anybody, whether they are a brand new believer or one who has been walking with God for a long time can have intimacy with God. You don't need to have an education to get alone with God and commune with Him, you just need to worship Him in Spirit

Your Cry For Intimacy

and in truth. You just need to have eyes to see His beauty.

> *Your eyes will see the King in His beauty; They will see the land that is very far off.*
>
> Isaiah 33:17

I believe one of the hardest things we will struggle with is learning to carve out time in our daily calendar to spend time with Jesus. It is much more difficult than it sounds. We have many things that get in the way. Our schedules seem to fill up fast, and we have so many responsibilities and demands on our time. But we must not allow other things (lesser pleasures) to get in the way. We must make a radical change with our schedules and give first priority to God Himself. Cry out and ask the Holy Spirit to help you. We want to be wise and live a focused life. Intimacy with Jesus will be the banner over our schedules. Let's not procrastinate. He is worth it all!

How many times have you found yourself saying: I just don't have time to get alone with God? I'm just too busy. Now do you actually buy into that lie? The problem doesn't lie in a lack of time, but a lack of priority. It's actually a lack of desire, because whatever you desire in life, you will pursue. Kind David is an excellent example of one who had a great desire to take a good look at God and discover His unsurpassing beauty.

> *One thing I have desired of the LORD, That will I seek: That I may dwell in the house of the LORD All the days of my life, To behold the beauty of the LORD, And to inquire in His temple.*
>
> Psalm 27:4

We must stop blaming the demands upon our schedule and start taking responsibility for the way we are living before the eyes of heaven. We must begin wrestling with a simple yet profound question: What is my life all about on the earth? What is eternal life? Once you settle that question inside your heart, you will begin to organize your life around it. I believe there is something inside you that is crying out to be near God's heart. There is a longing inside you to spend all your days getting to know how beautiful and tender God really is. Isn't that right? Eternal life is about a life of intimacy with God the Father and His Beloved Son.

> *And this is eternal life, that they may know You, the only true God, and Jesus Christ whom You have sent.*
>
> John 17:3

Nobody can change your lifestyle and schedule, not even your pastor or leader. You must be the one who makes the decision. You must be the one who acknowledges that you are bankrupt without the living flame of God's love inside your heart. This definitely includes me as well. It is our birthright to live as pilgrims on this earth, to be ruined for anything less than intimacy with God. Amen!

First Love

I am convinced that a life of intimacy is all about "first love." I believe this is what the Holy Spirit is highlighting in a very specific and focused way. All of heaven is shouting forth like a trumpet: return to your first love.

> *Nevertheless I have this against you, that you have left your first love.*
>
> Revelation 2:4

Only when we put Jesus first in our daily lives and let our passion be consumed with Him is it then called first love. One of the characteristics of first love is the desire to be as close as possible to the Beloved. First love is the one thing that is needful. We should desire it, pray for it and seek to attain it at all costs. Life becomes so meaningful and satisfying when our spirit becomes vibrant and buoyant on

Your Cry For Intimacy

the inside, and there's no greater feeling on earth than when our spirit begins to soar with God in the heights of glory.

We can't preach to others about first love if it doesn't grab us in such a way that anything less makes us miserable. We cannot put the Great Commission before the greatest commandment. Burnout is inevitable if we do. How can we effectively minister and impart life to others if we are not receiving life ourselves. The second commandment flows best out of the first. May we ask the Holy Spirit to produce a deeper cry in our hearts for Jesus Himself, and put into practice what we set our heart upon.

I believe this is why the Shulamite was crying out for the kiss of Jesus. She didn't want to have her love for God second, but first. She found her answer for the deep longing in her soul.

> *Let him kiss me with the kisses of his mouth—For your love is better than wine.*
>
> Song of Solomon 1:2

Jesus, the Bridegroom God, is filled with extravagant passion and beauty. Every other human love fades into nothingness. There is no one who can love like Him. It is why He yearns for our love and desires to take complete possession of us. He will not be satisfied until we give ourselves wholly unto Him. Divided love is of so little value to Him. He will not enter into a bond of love with such a soul. Jesus has the right to make such a claim upon our love, because there is no one so full of glory and so full of royal beauty as Him. He knows what He can bestow with His love. He knows how happy He can make a human soul. That is why He has a thousand times more right than any earthly bridegroom to say, "give me everything; give me your first love."

This is the calling and destiny for us as Shulamites. Remember, we are all Shulamites in pursuit of becoming a Bride. Wholehearted love is within our reach. It comes from Jesus Himself, because He first loved us. He has already planted the seed of love within our hearts. He first pursued us. He didn't wait for us to do something to move His heart, but His heart of love moved Him to do something. We have been empowered to become lovers of God's heart. We cannot draw back from this kind of relationship. We will fervently cry out to God to help us enter into a lifestyle of intimacy with Him. It will be worth it all in eternity!

How to Nourish Bridal Love

I believe we not only need to know more about what bridal love is but we need to learn how to cultivate and nourish it. This passionate love between Jesus and us must be continually nourished in order for us to have a dynamic and satisfying relationship with Him. Here are some simple keys of how to practice nourishing bridal love:

- To nourish bridal love we must practice the love of Jesus by uttering His name and adoring Him. Adoration is powerful. It's the words "I love you" that deeply move His heart. When we declare the name of Jesus, His glory begins to shine on us. When we speak of our Beloved often, we will be inflamed with love. His name is called "Wonderful Counselor, Mighty God, Everlasting Father, Prince of Peace" (see Isaiah 9:6).

- To nourish bridal love we must do everything "for His name's sake." What do I mean by that? It means that we are far more interested in how to make God happy than making ourselves happy. It means that every hidden motive inside of us is more focused on how to benefit God in whatever we do than benefiting ourselves. It is the words "for you" that have power. They are like wings transporting us to the One we love. As we do things for His name's sake, it makes difficult tasks easy. Your bridal love will be set aflame when you do everything together with Jesus all day long. Do the smallest and most ordinary things with Him and for His name's sake.

* To nourish bridal love we must practice a continual dedication to His will. Bridal love proves its genuineness here—the soul must submit itself continually to the will of God, even when we don't understand what He is doing and He frustrates its deepest wishes and desires. We do what He wants not what we want, even if it doesn't make sense. We must love Him while He is working in us. The flame of love blazes more fiery as we sacrifice our will upon the altar.

- To nourish bridal love we must meditate upon the sufferings of Christ. Jesus is the Man of sorrows. In heaven, He still bears His wounds and appears as the Lamb that was slain (see Revelation 5:6). He was wounded for love. We can only love Jesus if we have really taken His sufferings into our heart. The Cross is the greatest proof of true love. Love willingly treads the path of the Bridegroom, even if it is a path of thorns.

- To nourish bridal love we must long for our Lover to come back. When we are no longer expectant of Christ's second coming, the flame of our love will grow dim. When our thoughts center on His coming, we will sing of it and speak of it. This will bring Him closer to our heart and our love will increase. It is the Bride of Christ who will rule and reign with Jesus forever. He is coming back for a bridal partner. Hallelujah!

- To nourish bridal love we must receive a fresh revelation of the beauty of God. His beauty and majesty is so fascinating and exhilarating. The beauty of God shatters passivity! When the Spirit of revelation touches our spirit with how beautiful, tender, kind, patient and understanding He is towards us, especially when we keep stumbling, then bridal love will be awakened inside of us. Discovering God's beauty is my life vision. There is nothing that has transformed my life any more, except pain. Beauty and pain have been God's greatest tools to change me. I encourage you to go on a divine treasure hunt of searching out the depths of God's beauty. It will help nourish your bridal love.

The Reward of Intimacy

The greatest reward of having intimacy with God is a lovesick heart. The most powerful people on the earth, and the most dangerous people to the kingdom of darkness are those who are lovesick for the Bridegroom God. Lovesickness is birthed when our heart is tenderized by the love and fire of God's heart. The word "lovesick" is mentioned two times in the Song of Solomon:

> *Sustain me with cakes of raisins, Refresh me with apples, For I am lovesick.*
> Song of Solomon 2:5

> *I charge you, O daughters of Jerusalem, If you find my beloved, That you tell him I am lovesick.*
> Song of Solomon 5:8

To be lovesick means that absolutely nothing on earth can compare to your love for Jesus. There is nothing that can consume your soul like He does. He is the source and satisfaction for every hidden cry within (see Psalm 73:25). A lovesick person is fully satisfied yet always longing for more. You cannot manipulate or control a person in love. They cannot be bought because they serve without any price tags. A lovesick bride will embrace and endure anything for the sake of love!

I love to ask Jesus to grant me a lovesick heart for Him.

Your Cry For Intimacy

It is one of my primary prayers in life. It is my cry. But I know that it doesn't come so easily. Yes, it's the gift of God, but is also the one thing that He reserves very carefully. He will not cast a pearl before swine. I know He's watching the secret movements of my heart. I know that He only gives the deep things of His heart according to hunger. I know that it actually takes a tremendous focus to keep my heart alive in the power of lovesickness.

My greatest fear in life is that my hart would grow cold and hard on the inside. So, by the grace of God, I am determined to not allow this to happen. It is why I am focused on the life of the Shulamite in the Song of Solomon. It is why I am pursuing the fiery love of my Beloved. It's why I will keep crying out for the kisses of Jesus' love to deeply touch and impact my heart.

Questions to Ponder

1. How often do you cry out for the love of God to touch your heart? Would you make it a high priority in your life?
2. How often do you take the Bible passages from the Song of Solomon and sing God's affections over you?
3. How often do you say that you are just too busy and don't have time for God? What are you going to do about it?

CHAPTER THREE

The King's Chambers

Draw me away! We will run after you. The king has brought me into his chambers. We will be glad and rejoice in you. We will remember your love more than wine. Rightly do they love you.

Song of Solomon 1:4

The Shulamite received the divine kiss, but now she is about to receive a holy encounter with the King. Her cry is to be drawn away with Him. It's amazing!

The Shulamite Wants to Be Drawn

Do you notice the first three words she carefully prays? "Draw me away." She desires to be drawn away from the crowd. She wants to be free from any distractions that would hinder the love she so longed for and the love she encountered in Song of Solomon 1:2. She knows how her heart can be easily quenched by just being amongst the common crowd in the streets in Jerusalem. Remember, she is a farm girl who worked in a vineyard out in the hill country. She spent most of her time tending sheep, just like King David. She loved to be in the hills, worshiping her Beloved. That was her life vision. She had no desire to spend her time in downtown Jerusalem. She does love people, but she cannot afford to lose her high calling and destiny to be a radical lover and worshipper of the King.

The cry of "draw me" reveals the power and beauty in

the Shulamite's heart. It is her hidden cry that nobody sees but God Himself. It is her bridal cry shining in full radiance. "Draw me away" is her prayer of love and humility. She wants to be romanced by the King–that's her prayer of love, but she also knows that she needs help–that's her prayer of humility.

She understood her limitations in the grace of God. She knows that she cannot come before the King by herself. She wants to be ushered in and romanced by the King of the ages!

"Draw me" a simple yet profound prayer and cry of the heart. Many times I use the words "prayer" and "cry" as interchangeable. You cannot have a prayer life without having a deep cry inside, and you cannot have a deep cry without having a prayer life. They go hand in hand. There have been many times in my heart when I have prayed the prayer, "draw me Jesus." It seems so short, but it has great depth. Remember, we want to get the language of the Song of Solomon in our daily prayer life. Whenever God draws us, we must understand that He is taking us *from* something *into* something, from the natural realm to the Spirit realm. He's taking us directly to Himself. It is why He is producing the cry "draw me away" within each of us. When I prayer this prayer, I ask Jesus to draw me and escort me into the throne room of heaven. I want to be drawn away from the natural circumstances and into the realm of the glory of the King. The cry of "draw me" takes me from the outer court into the Holy of Holies. This is what "draw me away" means to me.

There are many Scriptures that talk about being drawn to God. Let us take a look at just a few of them.

> *Blessed is the man You choose, And cause to approach You, That he may dwell in Your courts. We shall be satisfied with the goodness of Your house, Of Your holy temple.*
>
> Psalm 65:4

The King's Chambers

Draw near to my soul, and redeem it; deliver me because of my enemies.

Psalm 69:18

Their nobles shall be from among them, And their governor shall come from their midst; Then I will cause him to draw near, and he shall approach Me; For who is this who pledged his heart to approach Me?' Says the Lord.

Jeremiah 30:21

The Lord has appeared of old to me, saying: Yes, I have loved you with an everlasting love; therefore with lovingkindness I have drawn you.

Jeremiah 31:3

I drew them with gentle cords, With bands of love, And I was to them as those who take the yoke from their neck. I stooped and fed them.

Hosea 11:4

No one can come to me unless the Father who sent Me draws him; and I will raise him up at the last day.

John 6:44

And I, if I am lifted up from the earth, will draw all peoples to Myself.

John 12:32

Many of these passages reveal what was in the heart of the Shulamite and they reveal what is in our hearts as well. We long to be drawn near the heart of God. We cannot be content to live at a distance like the Daughters of Jerusalem. Just as the Shulamite kept her prayer very simple and focused, so we will do the same. Just as she had a reaching heart, so we will have a reaching heart!

The Shulamite Wants to Run

Draw me away! We will run after You...
Song of Solomon 1:4

The Shulamite not only desires to be drawn away, but she wants to run after her Beloved. When she says that she will run after Him, it speaks of her wholehearted desire to be with Him. It speaks of her willingness to do anything for the sake of love. It speaks of her passion. She wants to be where He is and wants to do what He is doing. She is willing and ready to go wherever her Beloved wants to go. She basically wants to be swept off her feet.

I have always believed that running after God spoke of ministry. But now after praying this prayer more and more, I believe it reveals a cry and longing to be with God at all costs. That's the bottom line. When you fall in love with someone, you will run and put all effort to be with the person you treasure most. If God is in the secret place, then you will run after Him and find Him there. If God is up on mountains and wants us to do the works of the Kingdom, then we will run after Him and do what He wants us to do. Running after God is not about doing something, although that can be taking place, but it's about passion.

One of the best examples of what I am trying to communicate is the great picture of Peter and John the Apostle running to the tomb in John 20. After Jesus died and was buried, His body was taken by Joseph of Arimathea and Nicodemus to a tomb in a garden. The tomb was then sealed with a large stone that weighed over a thousand pounds. Two days later, Mary Magdalene went to the tomb with some burial spices, but to her surprise, she saw that the stone had been removed. So she immediately ran to find Peter and John to tell them what happened. It was a tremendous shock to them.

Once Peter and John heard this, they both ran to the tomb to see what happened. We are told that John outran

Peter. So what was going on here with Peter and John? I don't believe they had any concern for their own ministries or reputations while they were running. I believe they were caught up with the Man Christ Jesus and would do anything to find Him and be with Him. Yes, they were curious and wanted to see if the stone truly had been removed. But at the very core, they wanted to see if the One they loved and adored had truly risen as He said He would. They wanted to be His witnesses of an event that would change human history forever. They were so in love, that it swept them off their feet and caused them to run. Their running after God was all about passion!

Just like Peter and John, we want to run after our Beloved. We want to be found in hot pursuit of Him. But He will have to give us the legs to do it. It's called the spirit of grace. He must give us that enablement, that divine enablement.

The King's Chambers

After the Shulamite prayed to be drawn away and to run after her Beloved, she is immediately escorted into the King's chambers. Do you notice who it was that brought the Shulamite into the chambers? It was the King! This is the first face of God mentioned in the Song of Solomon. He is revealed as a King three times in the Song.

...The king has brought me into his chambers...
Song of Solomon 1:4

While the king is at his table, my spikenard sends forth its fragrance.
Song of Solomon 1:12

Your head crowns you like Mount Carmel, and the hair of your head is like purple; a king is held captive by your tresses (beauty).
Song of Solomon 7:5, emphasis added

You can see that the King has a private chamber which is designed to develop and equip the growth of the Shulamite's heart. That is why Jesus, the King, says that He is held captive by her beauty. He is producing something very precious inside her soul. He is fervently at work in her. It is why she is seen pouring and lavishing her love and perfume at His table (1:12). The perfume she experienced in Song of Solomon 1:3 is now being poured upon the King. It is why He takes the initiative to both draw her and then carry her into His private chambers. She has been favored in the eyes of heaven to minister to the King of glory in His private chambers.

The Hebrew word for "chambers" is *cheder*. It means innermost room, sacred place, pavilion and bridal canopy. It was a bedchamber that was separated by a curtain. It was a chamber within a chamber. It is not an ordinary place, but is a very sacred place. The chamber is a metaphor for prayer and sacred communion with the heart of the King. It is the Shulamite's private and hidden place that she treasures most. It's the place where she receives love and romance from the King. I believe the Good News Bible translation describes it best:

> *Take me with you, and we'll run away; be my king and take me to your room. We will be happy together, drink deep, and lose ourselves in love. No wonder all women love you!*
>
> Song of Solomon 1:4, GNB

This was the cry and prayer of the Shulamite, to be happy together, to romance in the King's chambers, to drink deep and to be lost in love. Selah!

It was the King who invited the Shulamite into His chambers. She had the cry to be drawn away, and the King heard her cry. It deeply moved His heart. He did what no other King would do; He called forth the one who has been overlooked, passed by and forsaken by others, and beckons

The King's Chambers

her to a place far superior to any earthly pleasure or glamour. He responded according to what was in her heart. And He will do the same for you and I.

Can you even imagine being invited by a king or president to spend quality time in their beautiful palace? There is no king who would open up their palace to just anyone. To have access into the secret chambers of a king you have to be somebody important or have great wealth and power. But this beautiful King is different. He is searching for something. Just as He released His kisses, so He longs for the kiss of the Shulamites (see Song of Solomon 8:1). He longs to be loved and admired. He is not just a King of power, but He's a King of love. The King is a lover. He is so humble, yet so passionate!

- The humble King came on a donkey into Jerusalem, heading to the Cross.
- The crowned King is coming back into Jerusalem on a white horse and taking over the entire earth.

The door to discover God's heart is wide open. Just as He ushered the Shulamite into His chambers, so He is inviting us to come and behold His kingly majesty and glory. He desires to draw us and invite us into His private chambers with Him. He wants us to come up and behold the throne room of heaven. The door to His heart is open—it's a season of grace.

> *After these things I looked, and behold, a door standing open in heaven. And the first voice which I heard was like a trumpet speaking with me, saying, "Come up here, and I will show you things which must take place after this."*
>
> Revelation 4:1

Being invited by the King into His transcendent palace is a huge statement of your worth before Him. Do you have any idea who you really are? Do I have any idea who I really am before Him? I think we are just beginning to have some understanding of our personal worth and value before the King. He is so committed to usher us into a confidence in who we are that we couldn't have even fathomed before. He really wants to restore our inner confidence in His chambers. He wants us to feel so important and special. He is the One who names us in His chambers as kings and priests before His throne (see Revelation 1:6). There is none like Him. He is destined to reveal His glory and He is destined that we walk in the revelation of His glory. This is the invitation into the chambers of a holy King!

Can you actually believe it? The King is not threatened or intimidated for His beloved ones to be near His throne. He actually insists that we be near Him to rule and reign with Him. To be in His chambers is to be near His throne. He longs to share His glory with us. He longs to share His throne. What king would share their throne with others? But it's His great delight and pleasure to do so (see Revelation 3:21).

The King not only wants to enthrone us, but He wants to crown us. The One who wears many crowns upon His head wants to crown us in His secret chambers.

> *Who redeems your life from destruction, who crowns you with lovingkindness and tender mercies.*
> Psalm 103:4

The King's chambers is a very intimate and private place. It's a place for divine encounter. Just as eastern kings allowed no one but their favored friends to their inner chambers, so the Bridegroom King allows no one into His chambers but His close friends. And we are His close friends–His favored ones!

The King's chambers is the secret place away from the crowd. It is where we can let down the walls of our heart and become very vulnerable and transparent. We can be

The King's Chambers

known for who we really are. We can pour out our troubled emotions to the heart of the King. I am reminded of Joseph, who when his brothers came to Egypt to buy food, saw Benjamin, his youngest brother, and was deeply moved. So he hurried out to look for a place to weep and went into his private room and wept there. After her came out, he washed his face and controlled himself.

> *Now his heart yearned for his brother; so Joseph made haste and sought somewhere to weep. And he went into his chamber and wept there. Then he washed his face and came out; and he restrained himself, and said, "Serve the bread."*
>
> Genesis 43:30–31

That is just one beautiful picture of what takes place in the King's chambers. Just like Joseph, sometimes you just can't control yourself and you need to find a private and personal place to weep.

The bridal chamber is the place to be still before the King. Just think how many inward voices arise inside our mind when we quiet ourselves before God? When the King brings us into the secret place away from the crowd, we begin to see the wilderness within our own souls. We see how spiritually barren we are. But the good news about the King's chambers is how this beautiful King fashions and establishes our core identity as a lover of God. It's who we are and it's what we do–forever! In the King's chambers we find out how special and favored we truly are. We are the ones the King delights in. We are the ones He rejoices over. We are the ones destined to abide in a place far superior to the spirit of this age. I believe we need to find out who we really are in the place of discovery, the King's chambers! It is in the King's chambers that we are given a new name and a new identity.

> *The Gentiles shall see your righteousness, And all kings your glory. You shall be called by a new name, which*

the mouth of the Lord will name. You also shall be a crown of glory In the hand of the Lord, And a royal diadem in the hand of your God. You shall no longer be termed Forsaken, Nor shall your land any more be termed Desolate; But you shall be called Hephzibah, and your land Beulah; For the Lord delights in you, and your land shall be married. For as a young man marries a virgin, So shall your sons marry you; And as the bridegroom rejoices over the bride, So shall your God rejoice over you.

Isaiah 62:2–5

Within the King's chambers is the banqueting table of Song of Solomon 2. The fulfillment of this will occur at the marriage of the Lamb (see Revelation 19:7–8). We will forever feast at His banqueting table. In fact, it's Jesus Himself who is going to gird Himself and personally serve us at His table. That's incredible! The King of the entire universe is going to stoop low and serve us as a servant.

Blessed are those servants whom the master, when he comes, will find watching. Assuredly, I say to you that he will gird himself and have them sit down to eat, and will come and serve them.

Luke 12:37

In the King's chambers, we discover that God's banner over our lives is love. It is not a banner of rejection; it's not a banner of failure; it's not a banner of fear. It's a banner of love. This is how the King defines us!

He brought me to the banqueting house, And his banner over me was love.

Song of Solomon 2:4

It is in the King's chambers that we remember that God's love is better than wine. That was the testimony of the Shulamite, as she declared; "we will remember your love more

The King's Chambers

than wine" (1:4). This is the second time she declares that Jesus' love is better than wine in the Song. Do you see yourself here? This is your journey that you are discovering. It's the very cry of your heart! It's the very cry of my heart. We will be the ones who have private times in the King's chambers that will change us forever. We will testify of His love. We will remember the times He marked us for Himself with His beauty, as He simply loved us as His Shulamites. To remember means we won't forget it. That's the great mark and seal of encountering the King in His chambers. To remember means that our gratitude will grow. Amen!

The King's chambers is our private time when our inner man is being formed and fashioned into Christ's likeness. It is not just about feeling good in His presence, but about us becoming His private garden. That's the divine working of the King's heart within our lives. We become a garden enclosed for Him. That means that no one else has access or entrance into the core affections inside of us. They belong to Him alone.

Spending time in the King's chambers not only benefits our relationship with God, but it benefits our relationship with others. When you go to work you have joy on the inside, you have strength on the inside and your heart is more alive. You are not so easily offended and bothered. You have more tolerance while under pressure. You actually get more work done and will break out with a smile while doing it. This is called being drawn and running after the King in divine partnership, and it's birthed in the chambers of the King.

May we learn to cultivate our own personal bridal chamber with the King, a place to romance with Him, that it would be a place to retreat and find refuge in the battle of the storm. Many of us are spending time elsewhere, and we are not spending personal and private time alone with the Bridegroom King. Our relationship will not grow if we don't. We must seek for it. We must have a big cry for a private chamber. The King who has many scars on His body and many crowns upon His head will be worth the time and struggle!

The Shulamite's Ultimate Joy

As we come to the end of this chapter, we find out the secret to the Shulamite's ultimate joy. We clearly see how her simple cry inside her heart to be drawn away and to run after her Beloved reached the heart of the King. It deeply moved Him. She confesses that she has a glad heart and a rejoicing heart.

> *Draw me away! We will run after you. The King has brought me into his chambers. We will be glad and rejoice in you. We will remember your love more than wine. Rightly do they love you.*
>
> Song of Solomon 1:4

We see that it was not what the Shulamite did that brought joy to her heart, but it was the person and presence of the King. He alone is her cause for rejoicing. Let us keep this in mind during our pursuit and journey in God's heart.

John the Baptist had a similar revelation. He was a true friend of the Bridegroom God. This mighty forerunner heard His voice. He found joy and delight in the wilderness. Listen to what he says:

> *He who has the bride is the bridegroom; but the friend of the bridegroom, who stands and hears him, rejoices greatly because of the bridegroom's voice. Therefore this joy of mine is fulfilled. He must increase, but I must decrease.*
>
> John 3:29

It was hearing the Bridegroom's voice that brought joy to his life, bringing delight even in the wilderness. If we are going to have a glad heart, especially in the seasons of the wilderness, we must learn to find our ultimate joy and pleasure in the heart of the King. He alone is the source of our

The King's Chambers

happiness, not our ministry or having perfect circumstances. We must cry out to Him like the Shulamite to be drawn away and escorted into His chambers and discover who He is as a King and who we are as His Bride. It's our destiny while upon the earth!

The words "be glad and rejoice" in Song of Solomon 1:4 is the same language of Revelation 19:7. And this gladness and rejoicing is all about a wedding.

> *Let us be glad and rejoice and give Him glory, for the marriage of the Lamb has come, and His wife has made herself ready." And to her it was granted to be arrayed in fine linen, clean and bright, for the fine linen is the righteous acts of the saints.*
> Revelation 19:7

The King wants to release a song in His chambers. It will be a song that captures and wins over the hearts of His Shulamites. It will be a song of deliverance and a song of rejoicing!

The Shulamite ends her prayer in Song of Solomon 1:4 almost exactly like she did in Song of Solomon 1:3. She says; "rightly do they love you." The New International Version says, "how right they are to adore you." Adoration is birthed in the King's chambers. It is right to love this beautiful King. He is worthy of our love and affections. He is worthy of our worship. He is worthy of our time and resources. Simply said: He is worth every pain and struggle we will ever face!

In the next chapter, we will see the Shulamite receive an incredible revelation of who she is to her Beloved. Up until this time in her journey, she has been discovering the beauty of the Bridegroom King, but now she is going to peer into her own soul and be stunned at who she is to Him. It's one thing to discover how awesome He is, but it's another thing to discover how awesome she is. It will radically change her love and devotion to the King.

CHAPTER FOUR

Facing Your Identity Crisis

I am dark, but lovely, O daughters of Jerusalem, Like the tents of Kedar, Like the curtains of Solomon.
                                              Song of Solomon 1:5

Now the Shulamite is going to receive two distinct truths of who she is to her King. Up until this point, all the revelation she has received has been of who her Beloved is. But now the revelation will shift to who she is in her journey to wholehearted love.

She declares with such boldness to the Daughters of Jerusalem that she is "dark, but lovely." This is very profound to her. I don't believe she borrowed this from a sermon, but it came directly from the heart of the King. It actually came from her time spent in the King's chambers. Remember, that is where she just became undone.

The Shulamite is giving us a priceless jewel right before our own very eyes. What she learned at the beginning of her journey can become one of our greatest possessions owned by our soul. We can have the balance of being dark and lovely to the King. Without this combined confession, we cannot fully grow into full maturity with the heart of Jesus. If we only see ourselves as dark and sinful, we become condemned. If we only see ourselves as lovely and mature, we become proud. We need the balance of both realities. Most of us don't have too much problem knowing that we are dark. It is why there is usually a cloud of discouragement and guilt in our lives.

But how many of us can actually believe that we are lovely to God, even when we blow it and not be filled with condemnation? It seems like the spirit of condemnation is flooding the minds of God's people. But Paul the Apostle tells us that we are not to give into this evil spirit because we are in Christ Jesus.

> *There is therefore now no condemnation to those who are in Christ Jesus, who do not walk according to the flesh, but according to the Spirit.*
>
> Romans 8:1

Let us first take a look at what the Shulamite was saying when she confesses that she is dark. I don't believe she is referring to the color of her skin. Yes, I realize she is a farm girl who worked out in the hot sun. But I believe she is describing the darkness and sinfulness of her inner life. The darkness refers to the perceived and unperceived areas of compromise that are hindering love with her Beloved. She says that she is dark and goes on and describes what being dark looks like. She says that she is dark just like the tents of Kedar, which were blackened, grayish tents made out of the dark skins of wild goats. The tents of Kedar speak of the darkness of the flesh, which is her first spiritual crisis that she is facing.

When she says that she is dark, she probably feels unworthy and has shame hovering over her life. Even though she had a great time in the King's chambers, she still can't escape the reality of her sinfulness. It follows her wherever she goes. She has to face the truth of what is going on deep inside her own soul.

How can she go from rejoicing in the King's chambers to declaring that she is dark? How can she suddenly go from being God–focused to being sin–focused in such a short time? What happened? The King is after something priceless within her heart. He wants her happy, but that is not His ultimate goal. The Shulamite is now being confronted

Facing Your Identity Crisis

with her identity and belief system. "Who am I," is the question she is facing. "Does the King still delight in me, even though I see myself as dark?" This is her identity crisis. This will be her great challenge to conquer. She knows that God's love is better than wine, but does she still have confidence in being His favorite one, knowing that she is dark and sinful?

The Darkness of the Flesh

God is committed to revealing the darkness and weakness of our flesh. It doesn't mean that He is trying to pick on us or make us look bad. Actually, He wants to keep us humble. It's His gift to us. He wants us to have a leaning heart at the end of our journey when we come up out of the wilderness (8:5). The Lord does not want us to stand in our own strength and commitment. He desires that we would find our confidence in His commitment to us and not our commitment to Him. That's the point!

God will reveal the darkness of our flesh, so we can set our hearts to agree with Him in each area He shines His light upon. He wants us to be holy as He is holy (see 1 Peter 1:16). He also yearns for nearness and fellowship and desires to share His life and heart with us. That is why He calls us to walk in the light as He is in the light.

> *But if we walk in the light as He is in the light, we have fellowship with one another, and the blood of Jesus Christ His Son cleanses us from all sin.*
>
> 1 John 1:7

We must face the reality of being dark. The flesh is weak, and we must accept it. There is a greater capacity for sin in our hearts than we really comprehend. No one fully grasps the depths of the wickedness of the human heart. Listen to what Jeremiah the prophet says.

> *The heart is deceitful above all things, And desperately wicked; Who can know it? I, the LORD, search the*

heart, I test the mind, Even to give every man according to his ways, According to the fruit of his doings.
Jeremiah 17:9

We must ask the Holy Spirit to search the depths of our inner man and be willing for Him to expose anything that is getting in the way of our devotion with the heart of Jesus. We have many unperceived areas of sin that lie undetected below the surface, just like hidden fault lines related to an earthquake. The human heart is very deceptive.

We must all face our identity crisis, just like the Shulamite. We must face the truth of who we are at the very core of our being. Let us lay aside the false masks that we wear, as we try to cover up who we really are. It's time for us to be real and transparent. May we begin to release the fear of being exposed that is tucked away in our hearts. I am really serious! There have been many times in my life when the Lord wanted to bring some emotional healing in me, but because of my fear of being exposed, I refused. As a leader, I didn't want anyone to see my weaknesses or look down upon me. As I ponder upon this, I totally regret it. God sees and feels my cry to be more transparent.

We believe what the Bible says in the passage in Jeremiah 17, but I don't think were fully convinced of it. It takes the power and person of the Holy Spirit to reveal what we cannot see. And it takes willingness on our part to allow God to search out the hidden areas of our lives.

Search me, O God, and know my heart; Try me, and know my anxieties; And see if there is any wicked way in me. And lead me in the way everlasting.
Psalms 139:23–24

Sometimes we are surprised when we commit a sin. We think because we are surprised by our sin, then surely God must be surprised. The question that we will continually ask is this: what is God thinking when we discover the

Facing Your Identity Crisis

weakness of our flesh? This is where the crisis begins. It is what the Shulamite had to face and conquer, as she discovered the darkness of her flesh. When we face the darkness of our flesh, we are actually facing a negative mindset in our thought life. This negative mindset is usually a master paradigm focus of how we view God in our thought life. We may not say it out loud, but it's what is happening in our daily thought patterns, especially when we stumble and fail before the Lord. We must shift our mindset from a master paradigm view of God to a bridal paradigm view of God. It's where we see Jesus as our Husband, and we see ourselves as the sons of God!

> *And it shall be, in that day, says the Lord, That you call Me My Husband, And no longer call Me My Master.*
> Hosea 2:16

> *Therefore you are no longer a slave but a son, and if a son, then an heir of God through Christ.*
> Galatians 4:7

If we don't focus on how lovely God is and how lovely we are to His heart, then we can form a negative mindset of thinking and only see ourselves as dark over a period of time. It can become very natural to always see ourselves in a negative way. It's called being dark–focused. And this dark–focus is usually more magnified when we find ourselves stumbling before heaven. It seems so difficult to sustain a constant belief of being lovely. But we must be careful that we don't get caught up into the spirit of guilt and condemnation when we face the darkness of our flesh, and we must be careful that we don't get caught up into the spirit of self–righteousness when we only see how lovely we are.

I believe one of the ways we can measure self–righteousness is by the amount of time it takes for us to feel totally clean and forgiven. If we start putting ourselves on probation for a season, then were giving into self–righteousness.

If it takes a whole week to have our confidence restored, then we must begin to study and pray the truths of how lovely we are to God, especially in the Song of Solomon. I believe we will begin to see a progression of going from weeks of guilt and shame to days, hours, and hopefully, minutes. We must embrace the combination of our darkness and loveliness together, just as the Shulamite is revealing to us in Song of Solomon 1:5. By knowing that we are dark to Jesus causes us to lean and draw upon His grace. By knowing that we are lovely, it produces a spirit of gratitude and gives us boldness to come before the throne of God.

> *Let us therefore come boldly to the throne of grace, that we may obtain mercy and find grace to help in time of need.*
> Hebrews 4:16

It seems like when we do fail the Lord, we always feel condemned. We think that God is very disappointed with us. We feel that He is losing His patience with us. But I don't believe that is the case for those who truly repent of their sin and declare war against it. God delights in showing mercy (see Micah 7:18). I believe when we fail the Lord, we miss His heart in the situation. We immediately focus upon our failure, rather than realize that God looks at us in every area of our life–both the good and bad. He sees the cry of our heart! It is very important that we ask God this simple question in our failure: Father, what do you have to say in this situation? We must ask Him and then wait for His voice. God far more understands the weakness of our flesh then we do.

Paul the Apostle, as a mature believer, understood the weakness of his own flesh. He described himself as chief among sinners (see 1 Timothy 1:15). This was not an exaggerated statement of false humility. Paul was a man who walked in the light and revelation of God's heart. That is where the increase of the darkness in his heart was revealed. If Paul embraced himself as being chief among sinners, then how about us.

The Lord knows so well our weaknesses and our strengths. I believe it's important for us to understand the weakness of our flesh–it keeps us humble. But it's also important for us to understand how lovely we are to God–it gives us confidence. But to take it even a step further, it is important for us to understand how much Jesus values our heart response to Him when we fail.

Lovely in the Eyes of the King

We are learning from the life of the Shulamite about the healthy two–fold confession of being dark, but lovely. We saw how God was so committed to reveal the darkness in her heart, but He's also committed to reveal how lovely she is to Him. Let us read the verse again and allow the Holy Spirit to bath us in the power of the truth.

> *I am dark, but lovely, O daughters of Jerusalem, Like the tents of Kedar, Like the curtains of Solomon.*
> Song of Solomon 1:5

The Shulamite testifies to the Daughters of Jerusalem that she is lovely. If she stopped after saying she was dark, it would be a long road ahead for her. But she didn't. She boldly confesses that she is lovely. And she goes on to describe what being lovely looks like. She says that she is lovely like the curtains of Solomon. The curtains of Solomon were the white curtains in the holy place in the temple. They speak of the inward work of grace in her life. The beauties of these curtains were hidden from the common person. Only the high priest could go into the holy place to see them.

The Shulamite was not only confronted in her belief system about her darkness, but she is being confronted in her belief system about her being lovely to the King. This will be the greater challenge of the two: being lovely–focused. This will give her confidence before her Beloved, especially when she fails Him. Because she has this revelation, she can come into the presence of her Beloved and feel no shame or condemnation. "Yes, I am dark, but He is treating me like I am so lovely. He is still loving me." This is her thought process regarding her perception of being lovely.

The Hebrew word for "lovely" is *na'veh*. It means beautiful, comely and adorable. This is the revelation that the Shulamite is receiving in her heart. She is beginning to believe that she is adorable, beautiful and lovely in the eyes of the King. All throughout the Song of Solomon, Jesus will tell her how lovely she is. He does this because it's His nature to do so, but also because He sees the big cry inside her heart.

I believe the revelation of being lovely in the King's eyes is one of the most powerful realities, yet it's one of the hardest ones to comprehend. It is one thing to *know* God's love for you, but it's another thing to *feel* His love for you. It is one thing to know you are lovely to God, but it's another thing to feel lovely to Him. What is very important for us to understand is that being lovely is not about how other people see us, but how God sees us. Beauty is in the eyes of the Beholder. God sees the end from the beginning. He sees us in light of the billions of years in which we will be perfect in love and obedience. You may not see anything in yourself that is desirable at this moment, but God does.

When I first heard a teaching by Mike Bickle, the director of the International House of Prayer in Kansas City, on the loveliness of the Bride of Christ, my heart was stunned that it was even possible. I never thought of myself as being lovely in God's eyes. To be perfectly honest, I usually felt dirty and unclean before Him. Now that doesn't mean that I was fooling around in the spirit of darkness, but I was actually pursuing the heart of God the best I knew how, with a spirit of love and devotion towards Him. I didn't have much of a problem seeing the Father in heaven as being lovely, but when it came to looking at myself, I never *believed* that I was beautiful and lovely. And to take it even a step further,

Facing Your Identity Crisis

I never *felt* lovely to God. I never felt His pleasure over me. I use to think that God could never be pleased or happy with me unless I was like Paul the Apostle; or I thought that when I died and went to heaven, then He would be pleased with me. This is a false paradigm of Jesus, the Bridegroom God. He is not so difficult to please. He's actually easy to please.

> *For whoever gives you a cup of water to drink in My name, because you belong to Christ, assuredly, I say to you, he will by no means lose his reward.*
> Mark 9:41

When you feel lovely to the heart of God, you become bold in your spirit. Is it possible to still feel confident in being lovely to God, knowing that we are dark inside? That's where we face our identity crisis. I believe it is possible to feel lovely to Jesus, even when we encounter the weakness of our flesh. It is very biblical to know that we are dark and sinful as the prophet Jeremiah described. But it's not the end of our story. It is only half–truth. We are more than just dark sinners. Do you understand who you really are in Christ Jesus? Do you know where your journey in God's heart is taking you? I am here to tell you that you are lovely and stunning to the Father of glory. You are absolutely awesome in His sight. You don't have to try and prove yourself to anyone. You don't have to gain a smile that you already have. When God looks at you, He doesn't just see all the negative things in your life, but He also sees the beautiful and positive things inside as well. This is a good time to say, Amen!

Listen to what Jesus speaks over the Shulamite after she received the truth of being lovely for the first time in Song of Solomon 1:5.

> *I have compared you, my love, to my filly among Pharaoh's chariots.*
> Song of Solomon 1:9

The horses that pulled Pharaoh's chariots were considered the very best in the world. They were big, strong, fearless and stunning in appearance. Solomon purchased them from Egypt for his special service and pleasure (see 1 Kings 10:28–29). These horses were chosen by and for the king alone. They were very costly. This is the revelation that Jesus is imparting over the Shulamite, as He develops the revelation of her loveliness to Him. He is telling her how lovely, strong and stunning she is to His heart. It was the word just for her!

Listen to what Paul the Apostle says about what is inside of every believer who loves God:

> *But we have this **treasure** in earthen vessels, that the excellence of the power may be of God and not of us.*
> 2 Corinthians 4:7, emphasis added

Do you believe there is a treasure inside you? Do you see the treasure inside of you or do you only see the earthen vessel? To consistently grow spiritually requires that we know how lovely to God we are, while in the process of discovering the darkness of our heart. There will always be a tension between both truths. But we must continue to press into the way Jesus sees us as His beloved. He does not despise our weakness as we so often imagine. He is not caught off guard by the stumbling of our flesh. He knows that we are a work in progress and wants us to know it as well. I believe deep inside our heart shines a light which the world cannot comprehend; the sound of melodies which cannot fade away.

God doesn't look at the outward appearance, but He looks at the heart. He sees the secret cry to love Him and obey Him.

> *But the LORD said to Samuel, "Do not look at his appearance or at the height of his stature, because I have refused him. For the LORD does not see as man sees; for man looks at the outward appearance, but the LORD*

Facing Your Identity Crisis

looks at the heart."
1 Samuel 16:7

God sees the cry of your heart! He knows that you are facing your identity crisis. What if He was to give you a radiant idea of who you really are in His eyes? What if you could see yourself the same way He sees you? You would feel ten feet taller. This is the place God wants to bring His Shulamites. When you see yourself so lovely and stunning to Jesus and you see yourself as His beloved, it takes you out of a negative mindset. You start becoming lovely focused. I believe this is the longing in your heart. Maybe you're asking the question: How do I begin to see myself as lovely to God? What do I have to do? I want to give you two simple; yet profound steps of how you can move into feeling lovely to the heart of the King. I'm sure you already have the truth of being dark conquered. Now it's time to know and feel lovely to Jesus.

Let me say that it will not happen overnight. It took you some time to get into this mess, and it will take some time to get out of it. But if you stay at it without quitting, you will get a breakthrough.

Two Simple Steps to Feeling Lovely to God

The first step to feeling lovely to God is: *understanding the righteousness of Christ that was imparted to us at Calvary.* We are made righteous and lovely to the heart of God through the finished work of the Cross. It is not our righteousness that makes us lovely, but Christ's righteousness in us.

> *For He made Him who knew no sin to be sin for us, that we might become the righteousness of God in Him.*
> 2 Corinthians 5:21

What a testimony–Jesus knew no sin. He was completely innocent. Even though He took upon Himself the sins of the world, He was completely free from sin and defilement. And because of His sinless perfection, we can find our true value and loveliness in Him. We will never know that we are lovely to God until we feel clean and forgiven by His blood. It's where we put our trust and confidence. We are to reckon ourselves as those who stand before God in the same righteousness that Jesus possesses. The beauty that we posses comes from the beauty that God possesses. Our loveliness streams from the glorious gift of Christ righteousness. Thank you, Jesus!

The ultimate definition of righteousness is that which is in accord with the nature and will of God. Righteousness is doing what is right. It is what is in the heart of God and who He is in His character as a person. Because of the finished work of the Cross, we are declared righteous before God as Jesus is. The Cross is more than legal acquittal. The Cross was a glorious, redemptive act of a passionate God who was willing to fight for the Bride promised by the Father. The Cross is Christ's righteousness, which cannot be improved upon. It is not something that is accomplished by man. It's a gift and work of the Man Christ Jesus. We are made righteous and complete in Christ. This is a legal truth declaring how we stand before God's court.

> *I will greatly rejoice in the LORD, My soul shall be joyful in my God; For He has clothed me with the garments of salvation, He has covered me with the robe of righteousness, As a bridegroom decks himself with ornaments, And as a bride adorns herself with her jewels.*
> Isaiah 61:10

It is Christ in us, the hope of glory which gives us the strong confidence and assurance of believing and feeling lovely to God the Father.

> *To them God willed to make known what are the riches of the glory of this mystery among the Gentiles: which*

Facing Your Identity Crisis

*is **Christ in you, the hope of glory**.*
Colossians 1:27, emphasis added

Our righteousness occurred instantly on the day we were born again. Every legal hindrance that would keep God from receiving us is removed forever. The innocent One became guilty, so the guilty ones could become innocent. Jesus Himself will present us holy and without blemish before the throne of God.

> *And you, who once were alienated and enemies in your mind by wicked works, yet now He has reconciled in the body of His flesh through death, to present you holy, and blameless, and above reproach in His sight.*
> Colossians 1:21–22

To be without blemish was the requirement of the sacrificial animal in the Old Testament. Jesus Himself will present us as a spotless lovely Bride to His Father. We simply cannot meet the demands of the righteousness of God–but Jesus can. He took our place. We have been cleansed by the blood of Jesus and forgiven through the cross. Forever we will be free from accusations, because accusations are what keep wholehearted love at a distance. God will finish the good work He started in us. He took my place down here, so that I might have His heaven up there. He did that for me!

> *He has delivered us from the power of darkness and conveyed us into the kingdom of the Son of His love, in whom we have redemption through His blood, the forgiveness of sins.*
> Colossians 1:13–14

Righteousness is not about any spiritual attainment–it is by faith. We need to have the understanding and confidence of our righteousness in the power of the blood of the Lamb. We can learn from the life of Abraham, as he was one who was declared righteous, simply because he believed. It wasn't how hard he tried or worked, but it was his simple faith.

> *For what does the scripture say? "Abraham believed God, and it was accounted to him for righteousness."*
> Romans 4:3

The second step to feeling lovely to God is: *knowing that we have a willing spirit inside of us.* I would call it a cry, a deep longing and desire deep inside your heart to fully abandon yourself to the heart of God. That's the essence of the Shulamite's cry!

God gave us an ability to cry out to love Him and do what is right, and He gave us an ability to choose evil and darkness. The choice belongs to us. It is important to understand that making decisions to love or to resist Jesus is not just a one–time thing He did. God put a yes in our spirit the day we accepted His Son into our hearts, the decision to fully love Him. Our willing spirit, which cries out for righteousness, must be cultivated during the rest of our spiritual journey. We must continually hunger and thirst for righteousness (see Matthew 5:6).

I believe at the very heart of our willing spirit is the deep hidden cry that only God sees. As I mentioned in the introduction, there is nothing more powerful than the cry you possess. It is your greatest weapon. God sees the sincere intentions to love and obey Him. It is important to understand that your sincere intentions to do right must be distinguished from spiritual attainment. God is looking at the cry in your heart more than the accomplishment and attainment itself. God relates to you according to the cry of your heart, and your simple follow through of obedience. He doesn't define you by your failure or by your accomplishments. He sees the desire and longing to become wholly His, even in your weakness. He sees the cry to change, even though you are still struggling with some issues in your heart.

Facing Your Identity Crisis

We must learn to understand how God feels about us now, even before we get the victory. Victory begins with a sincere cry to obey Jesus. That's where He sees you as being lovely to Him as the Shulamite described. He notices our inward desires and not just our outward actions. Every little yearning inside our heart to do right really matters to Him. Every movement of our heart toward righteousness is being recorded in heaven. He is the God who sees in secret.

But you, when you pray, go into your room, and when you have shut your door, pray to your Father who is in the secret place; and your Father who sees in secret will reward you openly.
Matthew 6:6

Not only does God see in secret, but He views things differently than man does. The King of glory sees something in you that nobody else sees. He sees you as a champion because a champion lives in you. When people look at you, they may only see a shepherd boy, but when God looks at you, He sees a king. He doesn't despise your weak love. He honors and values your cry to love Him, even while it's still growing and maturing. Hallelujah!

Two Great Examples of Men to Learn From

We have two great examples in Scripture of how God sees the hidden cry of the heart and calls forth His chosen ones. It was Gideon and King David.

In Judges 6, we have the account of Gideon. He was supposed to be out at war fighting the Midianites who were defeating the children of Israel. But he decided to stay back because of fear. Where was he when the Angel of the Lord appeared to him? He was hiding in the winepress, threshing the wheat at the bottom of the mountain. What did the Angel of the Lord say to him in this situation?

And the Angel of the Lord appeared to him, and said to him, "The Lord is with you, you mighty man of valor!"
Judges 6:12

The Lord saw in Gideon what he could not see in himself. God named him according to what he would become in the future. And we know that Gideon went on to become one of Israel's great military leaders. The King in heaven saw his cry!

What about the account of King David? He is another prime example of the grace of God. We know that he was a murderer and adulterer. He also struggled with pride as he was told not to take a census of his army. Yet, he went on and did it, showing forth his pride and arrogance. There are many other things David did that were not pleasing to the Lord. Yet, one thousand years after he died, listen to what God said about his life:

And when He had removed him, He raised up for them David as king, to whom also He gave testimony and said, 'I have found David the son of Jesse, a man after My own heart, who will do all My will.
Acts 13:22

God called David a man after His own heart. If God looks and rewards David like that, so will he do for us, for He never changes. If He saw the hidden cry inside his heart to fully do His will, so He sees the hidden cry inside of us to do His will. He sees what man doesn't see. He sees the cry to love Him with all of our heart and strength. It's lovely to Him!

I am so amazed at the grace and kindness of God's heart, as He relates to His people. He sees something we don't see. He sees something others don't see. Many of us are looking for someone to believe in us. We are looking for someone to call us forth. It is why we are so full of anger and disappointment. I believe when we stop looking to man to believe in us, the Lord Himself will call us forth. There is nobody who

Facing Your Identity Crisis 69

believes in you more than Jesus, the Bridegroom God. He is more than willing to call you forth into your destiny. Outwardly, people will see you as dark, but inwardly, the King of glory sees you as lovely.

As you study the life of the Shulamite, you can see tremendous progress in her being lovely throughout her journey. In 1:5, she declares that she is lovely like the curtains of Solomon. In 6:4, Jesus Himself now declares her beauty and says that she is lovely as Jerusalem. The Shulamite's glory of being lovely is developed throughout this eight–chapter love song. Here are the passages you can study to actually see this progression: 1:9–11; 2:1–2, 14; 4:1–5, 7, 10–11; 5:2, 9; 6:4–10; 7:1–7; 8:10.

One of the above passages that really amazes me about the Shulamite's confession of her loveliness is found in Song of Solomon 2:1.

I am the rose of Sharon, And the lily of the valleys.
Song of Solomon 2:1

She is beginning to change the way she thinks. "I am dark, but lovely" has now emerged into: "I am the rose of Sharon, and the lily of the valleys." The Hebrew word for "lily" is *shuwshan*. It was especially white, having six leaves, six petals, and six stamina. The snowy whiteness of its petals, its lofty stature reaching sometimes to four feet and a half, the delicacy of its form, and the uncommon elegance of all its parts cannot but strike every attentive observer with admiration. I believe the Shulamite was becoming convinced that she stood out amongst other lilies. She is starting to comprehend what her Beloved says about her. She is growing in her belief system. She is facing her identity crisis. She sees herself in the purity of a lily that grows in a dark valley. Something changes in her posture as she perceives that she is the object of the King's affections. This confession redefines her whole life.

I believe that it is essential that we are established in

knowing that we are the beautiful rose that God desires and cherishes. We are the ones who are lovely and stunning to the heart of God, because of the unique cry inside. A right image of a beautiful King produces a right image of ourselves, and a right image of ourselves produces a right image of others. When it dawns on us that we are God's rose, even in our vast weakness, something very powerful takes place on the inside. Yes, we are dark, but we are also lovely in the beautiful eyes of Jesus. Amen!

Our Eternal Destiny

We must always remember one of our ultimate core identities in God's heart. It is to be the Lamb's wife. Forever, we will be Jesus' lovely Bride, shining forth like a jasper stone.

> *Then one of the seven angels who had the seven bowls filled with the seven last plagues came to me and talked with me, saying, "Come, I will show you the bride, the Lamb's wife." And he carried me away in the Spirit to a great and high mountain and showed me the great city, the Holy Jerusalem, descending out of heaven from God, having the glory of God. Her light was like a most precious stone, like a jasper stone, clear as crystal.*
> Revelation 21:9–11

Questions to Ponder

1. When you discover the reality of your sinfulness, what negative thoughts come into your mind? What are you going to do about those negative thoughts?

2. Do you find yourself to be more dark–focused or lovely–focused when you look at yourself?

3. When you begin to realize that you are actually lovely in the eyes of the King, how does that make you feel? Why don't you take a few minutes and ponder what He says about you. Will you do that?

CHAPTER FIVE
Learning to be Still Before Jesus

Like an apple tree among the trees of the woods, So is my beloved among the sons. I sat down in his shade with great delight, And his fruit was sweet to my taste.
Song of Solomon 2:3

The Shulamite is describing her Beloved God as she compares Him to an apple tree. Just as an apple tree stands out amongst the trees of the woods, so He stands out amongst the sons of men. She is describing His beauty and His surpassing pleasure. Just as an apple is refreshing to the soul, so He is refreshing to the human heart. She is learning a great truth about Jesus as her Beloved, the One who is most sweet and refreshing to the soul!

She not only describes what her Beloved is like, but also describes what He can do to a human heart that discovers the depths of His emotions. She knows the great impact He is making in her own soul. She testifies of a powerful key from this encounter and shouts it forth like a trumpet. She declares, "I sat down in his shade with great delight." This is the very first time in the Song of Solomon where the Shulamite is pictured sitting down. The Hebrew word for "sat down" is *yashab*. It means to dwell, remain and to abide. This is what her soul longs for. She wants to abide and dwell under the glory of His heart. These are not just words coming from her lips, but it's something that is becoming very precious and priceless to her. The revelation of Jesus' love that she received in chapter 1 is beginning to sink in. She knows that stillness is not an automatic gift that comes from heaven, but it comes from divine encounter.

King David had the same revelation in Psalm 23. He encountered Jesus as His Shepherd and then was led to green pastures to lie down and rest. He was led beside still and peaceful waters.

> *He makes me to lie down in green pastures; He leads me beside the still waters.*
>
> Psalm 23:2

In Song of Solomon 2:3, we see how the Shulamite is learning to feast on the abundance of Jesus' beauty and sweet tenderness, as she's sitting under the apple tree with great delight in her heart. She can just sit in the presence of His glory and do nothing but receive. Simply put, she is a happy camper! We find out in chapter 8 that it was Jesus, the Beloved, who was awakening the Shulamite under the apple tree.

> *...I awakened you under the apple tree...*
>
> Song of Solomon 8:5

The Shulamite is learning one of the hardest things for a human being, and that principle is learning how to be still and do nothing in the presence of her Beloved but receive. That is why her heart was being awakened. It is what helped her to settle down and sit still. She knew that it was not about trying harder, but receiving more. She is teaching us a valuable lesson of being still and resting under the shade with her Lover. When she uses the word "shade" she is referring to the Cross. The work has already been finished at Calvary, and she can sit under the completeness of it. Let's read the verse again and understand what is happening with the Shulamite in this season of her journey.

> *Like an apple tree among the trees of the woods, So is*

Learning to be Still Before Jesus

my beloved among the sons. I sat down in his shade with great delight, And his fruit was sweet to my taste.
Song of Solomon 2:3

The Struggle to Be Still

Do you notice that after she testifies of her Beloved, the One who stands out among the sons, she says; "I sat down." This reveals her sincere encounter under the apple tree. She learned another valuable lesson in her pursuit of wholehearted love: being still. One of the most difficult things we will face in our Christian walk is the art of being still in God's presence. We are living in a busy generation, and the pace is tremendously fast. Learning to be still and rest in the presence of God has always been a struggle in my walk with God. I have always been a very active person. I am the youngest of six children and was the most spoiled. My mom would always say to me, "Mike, you are too hyper." She was definitely right! I had so much energy, and the only way I could release it was through sports. I played almost every sport growing up and was involved in a lot of competition. Winning was the goal. So here I am, a person who is very active and driven by performance.

I have realized that when I get too busy and don't take time to be still and rest, I become easily irritated and bothered. By the grace of God, I am learning a whole new lifestyle before heaven. I am learning that stillness and doing nothing is a place of strength for me. I'm learning that if I cease striving, then God will take over. But it is not as easy as it sounds. The flesh is very active and does not want to be subject. It wants to rule. It wants to be king. But I know that if I cultivate a lifestyle of stillness, the flesh will become subject to my spirit (see Romans 8:13).

Stillness produces God consciousness. When we sit still in the presence of the King, He will take us places in His heart to discover. He will usher us into the banqueting table, just like He did for the Shulamite.

He brought me to the banqueting house, And his banner over me was love.

Song of Solomon 2:4

If we are honest, many of us don't know how to be still and sit at the banqueting table with our Beloved. We are always fidgety. We are looking for some activity; something to do. We like to be on the run. But that is not the case for a bride on her wedding day. When she is being fitted for her wedding gown, she must be still and not move around. There is no such thing as a bridal dress with track shoes. Resting and stillness is where we find security in the heart of Jesus and we receive His affirmation. It is where we learn to feel enjoyed by the God of all beauty. Basically, we can't really be still until the heart is satisfied in God. We must cultivate a lifestyle of waiting upon the Lord in every season in our journey.

But those who wait on the Lord Shall renew their strength; They shall mount up with wings like eagles, They shall run and not be weary, They shall walk and not faint.

Isaiah 40:31

There are so many of God's people who are overworked and facing burnout. The demands upon their work and ministry seems to increase as time goes by. I have met many spiritual leaders who told me how busy their schedule was. I am sure you and I can relate. We can go on and on about the pressures that are staring at us right in the eyes, but I don't believe that is the real issue. The real issue we are facing is a heart issue, period. There are no excuses for anyone. We cannot blame the demands of our work or the demands of the church. Stillness is not just a flesh problem but also a heart problem. The reason why our flesh gets restless is because our heart is restless. We must learn to still our hearts under the apple tree with our Beloved God. The revelation of a 'tender Father' and a 'cherished Bridegroom' will help

Learning to be Still Before Jesus

settle the restless soul within us.

Learning to be still is an art, and it will begin to take place when we stop trying to perform. If you are a person who has always had to perform to gain acceptance and approval, then you will definitely have a difficult time being still. But I don't believe you need to feel discouraged. The Lord so desires to help you in the process. He sees your cry and longing to want to be still. He will personally teach you how to quiet your soul before Him and when you do, you soon discover that you're no longer searching for acceptance.

The Need to Perform

Performance is not about what we do, but why we do things. It is the hidden motivation of the heart. I believe many of us are trying to perform to earn love and gain acceptance in the eyes of men, especially with leaders.. The message underneath the surface is this: "I will not be loved unless I earn it." We may not admit that we feel this way, but we must allow God to shine His light upon us and reveal to us what He sees. We must realize that so much of our motivation is driven by fear of rejection. It's driven with a need to be needed and a need to be complimented or seen by some spiritual leader. For me, as a leader, I have failed in this area so many times. But I'm willing to learn. It is important for us to understand that performance is striving being manifested! It's a heart not at rest with the God of all beauty. It is restless on the inside, searching for something to fill its void. King Solomon understood this truth.

> *"Vanity of vanities," says the Preacher; "Vanity of vanities, all is vanity." What profit has a man from all his labor in which he toils under the sun? ...I have seen all the works that are done under the sun; and indeed, all is vanity and grasping for the wind.*
>
> Ecclesiastes 1:2–3, 14

What we are facing in our generation is this drive of having to do something to cover up our hidden pain. We think the busier we are, especially in ministry, the more God must be pleased with us. We seem to have this inner urge to always have to accomplish some task. It makes us feel better about ourselves. Now I am not saying we should be inactive and do nothing at all. The Book of Proverbs communicates the reward of a hard and diligent worker. It's important that we understand the different seasons that God has tailor-made for each one of us. God has called us to rest and be still and to partner with Him in ministry.

One thing that I have learned in my walk with God regarding being still is this: I can't fully bond to God's heart without first being still before Him. This is especially true when the pace begins to pick up and I begin to get very busy. There is something dynamic that takes place in my heart when I learn to quiet myself down and allow my Beloved to just come and love on me. That's where the true bonding takes place. It takes time to get to know what God is like. It takes time to understand His ways and build a history with Him. I believe we can learn the art of being still before Jesus, the Bridegroom God, just like the Shulamite was doing in Song of Solomon 2:3, when she sat down and rested under the apple tree.

If we don't sit before Jesus in stillness and be intimate with Him, then we neglect the one thing that matters most to Him, which is the garden of our heart. The Song of Solomon calls it our own vineyard. I believe the Shulamite learned this lesson well. If you go back to Song of Solomon 1:6, you see her struggle as she neglects the most precious thing to Jesus. Just listen to what she says and may we learn from this lesson where she failed.

> *...My mother's sons were angry with me; They made me the keeper of the vineyards, But my own vineyard I have not kept.*

Learning to be Still Before Jesus

Song of Solomon 1:6

The Shulamite was so busy keeping everybody else's vineyards that she doesn't keep her own vineyard. The vineyard represents her heart. Her gaze gets off the love of God. The Mother's sons represent the leaders in the Body of Christ who make her very busy. They overload her with many tasks, and she doesn't know how to say no to them. But it dearly costs her. They are more work–focused than heart–focused. They gave her an identity as a worker and not a lover. She is supposed to be in the King's chambers, but she's tending the garden of others while neglecting her own vineyard.

But the good news is how she quickly recovers from this mistake and finds her answer in 2:3. She not only sits down before her Beloved in stillness, but she sits with great delight. It isn't a burden to her–it is a great joy and delight. She is now tending and keeping the garden of her own heart. Let us read again and see that she is now doing her heart's cry and not fearing or pleasing man.

> *Like an apple tree among the trees of the woods, So is my beloved among the sons. I sat down in his shade with great delight, And his fruit was sweet to my taste.*
> Song of Solomon 2:3

I believe the Holy Spirit is teaching and training His Shulamites the art of stillness, even in the midst of great difficulty and pressure. It is something He is very jealous over. He will help us in our weakness. He knows our struggle to be still and do nothing. He knows that we think we have to do something to get His attention. Maybe we have tried every ministry conference that's out there to find healing, but we still seem to be stuck in prison. I want to suggest and encourage you to try and learn the principle of Song of Solomon 2:3 and give it some time. You have tried everything else, so why not give it a chance? You have nothing to lose!

I am convinced that true inner healing comes when the heart is still and quiet. It's not the only way, but it's the primary way. When we are not still we can't get into the core pain in our soul. We must slow down and learn to bond our heart to God's heart, and turn our attention to the Holy Spirit who dwells inside of us. A person who can't be still is a person whose heart is wounded and their soul is empty of love. It's called a love deficit. The answer is not doing more things, but coming before the Lord and allowing Him to settle the heart down in His love. If you struggle to be still and quiet, then I want to encourage you to pray the passage in Zephaniah 3 over and over until you find your soul at rest and at peace.

> *The Lord your God in your midst, The Mighty One, will save; He will rejoice over you with gladness,* **He will quiet you with His love**, *He will rejoice over you with singing."*
>
> Zephaniah 3:17, emphasis added

The prophet of God gives a secret to having a happy heart in this passage. He tells us that it's the Mighty One who rejoices over us with gladness and who will quiet us with His love. He is a master at doing this. He knows how to still the heart. He knows that when He quiets and calms the inner world, He then can shout forth and sing His love songs over us. He can rejoice over us with His happy heart!

As we are studying the life of the Shulamite sitting under the apple tree with great delight, I want to look at a wonderful, but challenging passage that directly relates to it. Are you ready to begin the process and master the art of being still and calm right now?

A Calm and Quiet Soul—Psalm 131

Psalm 131 is an incredible Psalm that relates to stillness and quietness. Just as the Shulamite learned to sit down, so King David learned to quiet his soul. Psalm 131 and Song of

Learning to be Still Before Jesus

Solomon 2:3 definitely go hand in hand.

Psalm 131 was written by David in his younger days before he was anointed king by Samuel, the prophet. It is one of the shortest Psalms to read, but one of the longest to learn. It is like a short ladder yet rises to great heights. This psalm gives us some keys to help us learn how to be still under the shade of God's presence. As we read this Scripture together, let's approach it as if we have never read it before. Does that sound good?

> *Lord, my heart is not haughty, Nor my eyes lofty. Neither do I concern myself with great matters, Nor with things too profound for me. Surely I have calmed and quieted my soul, Like a weaned child with his mother; Like a weaned child is my soul within me. O Israel, hope in the Lord from this time forth and forever.*
>
> Psalm 131:1–3

David learned the same principle as the Shulamite. He learned to calm and quiet his soul before God Himself. He learned a lifestyle of stillness. Now obviously, he didn't learn this overnight. We know how difficult it is to cultivate this type of lifestyle. So what was the key for David? What did he understand from heaven that helped him speak with such confidence about calming and quieting his soul like a weaned child to God's heart? I believe the answer is found in the very beginning of the verse. He says that his heart was not haughty or proud. Now I don't believe that David was being proud or exercising false humility when he said this. When David talked about a proud heart, he was not just referring to a person who loves the spotlight and wants to be the unique one amongst the crowd, but he's referring to a person who is self–sufficient, self–dependant, and one who exerts a lot of his own strength to serve God.

I can definitely relate to this, because I have always been one with a strong will. I have spent so many years pursuing

God's heart yet exerting my own strength and energy. How many times have I caught myself trying to figure things out, leaning to my own strength. I was not like a weaned child totally trusting and resting under the embrace of a passionate God. Neither was I like the Shulamite, sitting under the apple tree with great delight. It was in my own strength that I was trying so hard to please God. I was not surrendering myself in complete dependence upon the Lord.

The heart gets very restless and proud when things don't go our own way. A proud heart cannot rest! We can never meet God when we are striving or trying to make something happen in our own strength and zeal, but only when we begin to feel settled and rested on the inside. It's there where we will meet our Lover.

David not only said that his heart was not proud, but he said that he didn't concern himself with great matters. This was another key lesson he learned.

Neither do I concern myself with great matters, Nor with things too profound for me.
Psalm 131:1

What a testimony! David found a place in God's heart where all the troubles and concerns in his soul disappeared. He knew how to cast all of his burdens, those things that were precious to him, upon His God. He was a man of great peace. He was a man of rest. If we are going to walk with God with a humble heart, we must not concern ourselves with great matters. And this can mean so many different things for everyone of us. We are not to worry about our future ministry. We are not to worry if we will be promoted in leadership. We are not to be worried if we will ever get married and have a partner in life. We are not worry about our health. We must learn to surrender our concerns every day, and become like a weaned child, totally resting and enjoying the presence of our heavenly Bridegroom. Peter tells us to cast all of our cares upon the Lord because He greatly cares for us (see 1 Peter 5:7). Now I know it's not as easy as it sounds. But there is a way of victory in the Spirit. There is a place in glory where we can learn what David and the Shulamite learned.

Let us learn from David's life the secret to having a humble heart that doesn't concern itself with great matters, becoming like a weaned child within our souls. Amen!

Listening to God in Silence

Let us read the passage again in Song of Solomon 2:3. It never hurts to be repetitive reading Scripture.

> *Like an apple tree among the trees of the woods, So is my beloved among the sons. I sat down in his shade with great delight, And his fruit was sweet to my taste.*
> Song of Solomon 2:3

When the Shulamite sat down under the apple tree, she is not only learning to be still before Him, but she is learning another very important thing in her spirit. She was learning to listen to the voice of the Bridegroom. It's one thing to be still and silent before God, but that is not enough. Being still is for the very purpose of clearly hearing the voice of God. We are not being still just to be still. We are being still with a focused purpose, and that purpose is to connect our heart with God's heart. We are positioning our hearts and minds to hear His glorious voice. Being still is good, but being still and hearing the voice of God in your heart is better. We must not only learn the art of being still, but we must also learn the art of listening to God's voice.

Now obviously, there is nothing in Song of Solomon 2:3 that says anything about God's voice. So how do we know for sure that she heard the voice of the Sovereign King? I can't prove it, but the Shulamite does testify that she had great delight under the apple tree. That means she was really happy on the inside. Yes, she probably felt His presence, but I believe she heard His glorious voice while sitting down under His shade.

I can personally testify to this in my own life. As I have walked with God for almost twenty years, I have had the privilege of hearing God's voice. He has spoken to me many different ways, for it's His great pleasure. As I look back to each time He spoke, most of what I heard from Him was in complete silence. I am not saying that God can't speak to us while on the run. But I can identify the most powerful and clearest times I did hear the voice of the Bridegroom—it was when I was sitting still before Him and just adoring Him. Feeling His presence brought delight to my heart, but hearing His voice brought *great* delight to my heart.

Many believers have made hearing the voice of God so difficult. They are not accustomed to think that God speaks to a person's spirit. Instead, they imagine they are merely thinking their own thoughts. I have listened to one grand theme coming from their lips, and that is: "I just don't hear the voice of God for me personally." Now I understand there are times when we may not hear God's voice so clearly, but as a rule in our lives this should not be the case. The writer of Hebrews tells us that God has been speaking to His people through His Son (see Hebrews 1:2).

Can you imagine what it is like to hear the voice of God who is incredibly happy? (see Zephaniah 3:17). Imagine the dramatic effect the sound of consistent happiness can have upon a human heart. The voice of God is powerful and full of glory and majesty. He does speak, He does have a voice and He thunders from His pavilion. The God of glory thunders! He roars from on high. Listen to what is said about the voice of God in Job 37. It's powerful!

> *At this also my heart trembles, And leaps from its place. Hear attentively the thunder of His voice, And the rumbling that comes from His mouth. He sends it*

forth under the whole heaven, His lightning to the ends of the earth. After it a voice roars; He thunders with His majestic voice, and He does not restrain them when His voice is heard. God thunders marvelously with His voice; He does great things which we cannot comprehend.

Job 37:1–5

It is a simple revelation–God speaks! So the problem is not with God speaking, but with us not listening. God doesn't restrain the majesty of His voice. Jesus said that His sheep do hear His voice (see John 10:4). We have not taken time to cultivate a listening heart and deep communion with the Bridegroom God in our personal lives. We have too much clutter in our minds and seem to be more focused upon our current problems than Jesus Himself. Instead of blaming God and accusing Him for not wanting to speak to us, we should learn to take more time to listen for His voice in complete silence. That is our responsibility. The most practical and foundational way to hear the voice of the Beloved is through the Word of God, and a life of contemplation, or listening prayer.

We keep ourselves from hearing God's voice when we do most of the talking. It's a one–sided relationship. How long do you wait for a reply when lifting up your prayer request to the Lord? Do you wait a minute? Do you wait five minutes? Would you ever wait in silence thirty minutes or more?

Let us begin to cultivate a listening heart and believe that Jesus loves to speak to His Shulamites. He didn't passionately bring us into a holy and unique relationship with Him and then decide to back off and be passive toward us. Remember, He is so beautiful and stands out among the sons of men, just as an apple tree stands out in the woods. He wants us to partake of His fruit, sitting under the apple tree.

Jesus will keep pursuing us and He wants us to keep

pursuing Him in silence. Do we understand that silence is a pursuit? Let us be a people who positions our hearts in stillness to hear the voice of the Bridegroom. Let's be a bridal generation who clearly recognizes the voice of the Beloved, and ministers to His heart before His banqueting table.

Three Simple Lessons we Learned

1. We must be still and rest with great delight under the apple tree as the Shulamite did in Song of Solomon 2:3.
2. We must be comfortable with doing nothing in God's presence but receive.
3. We must quiet down our hearts and connect with God's heart to hear His voice.

As we come near the end of this chapter, I want to take a look at the rest of Song of Solomon 2, which is very important in the Shulamite's journey. It will give us more clarity for when we come to chapter 3. Remember, this is your story. It's your journey that you are discovering in the Song of Solomon. It is the cry of your heart!

Jesus Beckons the Shulamite to Arise

The Shulamite just learned how to enjoy being still under the apple tree in Song of Solomon 2:3. We see in the next verse that she also sits at Jesus' banqueting table, beneath the banner of His love. But now Jesus beckons her to arise from this place of rest and wants her to go up on the mountains with Him. Jesus' call is for her to leave her comfort zone and partner with Him in places she's never been. Please take some time while reading over this incredible passage in Song of Solomon 2.

> *The voice of my beloved! Behold, he comes leaping upon the mountains, Skipping upon the hills. My beloved is like a gazelle or a young stag. Behold, he stands behind*

Learning to be Still Before Jesus

our wall; He is looking through the windows, Gazing through the lattice. My beloved spoke, and said to me: "Rise up, my love, my fair one, and come away. For lo, the winter is past. The rain is over and gone. The flowers appear on the earth; The time of singing has come, And the voice of the turtledove is heard in our land. The fig tree puts forth her green figs, And the vines with the tender grapes Give a good smell. Rise up, my love, my fair one, And come away! "O my dove, in the clefts of the rock, In the secret place of the cliff, Let me see your face, Let me hear your voice; For your voice is sweet, And your face is lovely." Catch us the foxes, The little foxes that spoil the vines, For our vines have tender grapes. My beloved is mine, and I am his. He feeds his flock among the lilies. Until the day breaks And the shadows flee away, Turn, my beloved, And be like a gazelle Or a young stag Upon the mountains of Bether.
Song of Solomon 2:8–17

This is the glorious song that burns deeply in the heart of the Beloved. He is not just speaking this to the Shulamite, but He is singing it. It's a part of the song of all songs. In this forerunner song, Jesus is pictured as leaping and skipping over mountains. The mountains speak of the places of difficulty that hinder faith and obedience. Jesus shows Himself as the Sovereign King. He wants her to arise with Him to the mountains. He does not want her to just sit under the apple tree all of the time. He wants her to arise from what was familiar to her and step out in faith, trust His perfect leadership, and follow Him to the nations of the earth. It doesn't mean she won't have times of being still and resting in His presence, but it is a new season of her journey, and she has much to discover about who her Beloved really is. The key question she faces is this: can He be fully trusted in what He is calling her to do?

Jesus is awakening her heart to a new season. It is the same voice she heard before, but with a new message. The passage says, "Behold, He comes" (2:8). The word "behold" is used to signal her attention. Something very dramatic and definitive is being communicated to her.

I like the word picture that the Shulamite uses regarding her Beloved. She says that He is like a gazelle (2:9). Gazelles are known as swift animals that can reach high speeds of 50 mph for long periods of time. They are beautiful deer that can effortlessly climb mountains and leap over hills. They are swift in their sudden, energetic movements. This is what reminds the Shulamite of her Beloved. He has absolutely no problem walking upon and conquering the mountains in her life, those circumstances that are difficult to maneuver. Maybe her problems and difficulties seem huge in her own eyes, but to Him they are just little stepping stones that He can leap over and conquer. She is being invited to the high places with Him.

Jesus, as a gazelle, can leap over the mountains with no problem, but He invites the Shulamite to come along with Him. If He can effortlessly leap and skip over mountains, then so can she. As long as she is with Him, she will have no problem facing the dangers and difficulties. Jesus wants her to develop a personal history in His faithfulness. He wants her to be secure and feel safe with Him. He desires that she would have a strong and deep foundation of trust inside her heart. He is the Sovereign God and has all authority and wisdom over the dangers in her life (see Daniel 4:34–35).

Even though it's a time for her to leave her comfort zone, we must remember that it is a season of singing. It's a time of enjoyment and a season of fruitfulness (2:12–13). It is a time for her heart to rejoice in what her Beloved is doing in their relationship. It's a new season for her!

In this song, we see one distinct cry from Jesus to the Shulamite. He says, "Come away with Me." He says it not only once, but twice.

Learning to be Still Before Jesus

My beloved spoke, and said to me: Rise up, my love, my fair one, And come away...Rise up, my love, my fair one, And come away.
Song of Solomon 2:10, 13

At this point, Jesus is up on the mountain and the Shulamite is down in the valley. He is looking down at her. He wants a partner and a friend to go with Him to new places in His heart. It is a divine invitation from heaven to the Shulamite. It is all about partnership. He wants her to learn and take risks with Him. He wants her to be so utterly dependent upon His perfect leadership. But the sad news is that she is not willing to leave her comfort zone and arise with her Beloved to the mountains. She refuses to come away with Him. She decides to stay at the bottom of the mountain. Just listen to what she says to His divine proposal:

Until the day breaks And the shadows flee away, **Turn, my beloved**, *And be like a gazelle Or a young stag Upon the mountains of Bether.*
Song of Solomon 2:17, emphasis added

Do you notice the key word here? It's the word "turn." The word turn in the Hebrew literally means "the separation." As long as He was with her in the safety of His chambers, she could never stand to be apart from Him. But when the dangers of the mountains are suggested, she comes to even desire separation from Him.

Jesus wants her up on mountains with Him. That is His desire! However, because of her fear and immaturity, she is afraid to step out of her comfort zone and live by faith. She was enjoying sitting under the apple tree. But this is not where she is supposed to be in this season. She is afraid and is not being fully obedient to the Lord by saying yes. She is the one who told her Beloved to turn. Her fear is her disobedience, but it's not her rebellion. That's very important to understand. I believe you can most likely relate to the Shulamite here. How many times has God called you to go somewhere or do something that was uncomfortable to you, and you refused? You were unwilling to launch out by faith. I strongly believe that it was your hidden fear and broken trust that caused you to say no, but it wasn't any form of rebellion. In fact, as you pondered over it for some time, you regretted it. That was your cry shining forth like a bright light to the heart of God. Hallelujah!

In the next chapter, we are going to see how Jesus, her Beloved, responds to her refusal to go to the mountains with Him. Song of Solomon 3 is a fantastic chapter to learn from. Before turning to the next page, see if you can guess what happens to the Shulamite.

CHAPTER SIX

The Discipline of God

By night on my bed I sought the one I love; I sought him, but I did not find him. "I will arise now," I said, "And go about the city; in the streets and in the squares I will seek the one I love." I sought him, but I did not find him. The watchmen who go about the city found me; I said, "have you seen the one I love?" Scarcely had I passed by them, When I found the one I love. I held him and would not let him go, Until I had brought him to the house of my mother, And into the chamber of her who conceived me.

Song of Solomon 3:1–4

You guessed it! The Shulamite is being disciplined because of her refusal to go to the mountains with her Beloved. What a contrast between chapters 2 and 3. In chapter 2, we just saw how content and peaceful she was while sitting under the apple tree. But here in chapter 3, she is not at peace. She has lost the manifest presence of God in her life. She has lost the one thing she desired most, and that's the sweet presence of the Beloved!

Understanding the Discipline of God

This is the very first time the Shulamite is disciplined by her heavenly Bridegroom. It was just a short time ago that she was enjoying His sweet presence, but now things have suddenly changed. She learned the principle of tending the garden of her heart earlier, and now she is about to learn to embrace the principle of God's discipline.

I think we all have a general idea of what God's discipline is, but let's look at it in more detail. *The All Nations Christian Home and School Dictionary* defines the word discipline as:

- Training that produces obedience, self–control or a particular task
- Control gained as a result of this training
- Training (sometimes painful) that corrects, molds or perfects

For me personally, I have always struggled with the discipline of God. Even though I know the Bible passages and believe that God's discipline is His love, I have had a wrong mindset of it. Every time I was disciplined growing up, I was punished with a wrong spirit. It wasn't so much with my parents, but with my school teachers, coaches, and the employees I worked with. Just one little mistake and then would come the strict punishment. It produced a deep fear and anger in my heart. There was no grace or patience shown to me when I made a mistake. This became a normal mindset and expectation for me. After years of having this mindset of what I thought discipline is, I began to fear making any type of mistakes. I felt like I had to be perfect in everything that I did or I would pay the price for my mistake. It definitely built a performance mentality within me, and I operated more in fear than love. I had much to learn in the school of God's loving discipline.

Now before we look more in detail at the discipline of God, I do want to make clear that even though we had people, or possibly parents in our life who didn't model what true discipline is, we are still fully responsible for our response and attitude towards God's discipline. It's God who is passionately after our heart, not man. We can't allow others to dictate in a negative way what God's heart looks like. Our response is our responsibility. We must learn to separate the ungodly actions of man from how we respond. That's very important!

As we look at discipline, we must know the difference between discipline and punishment. They may seem like they are the same thing, but they are not. The New International Version translation does use the word punishment in Hebrews 12, but I don't believe it's the correct word. Punishment involves fear. It's feeling like you are going to pay a price for your mistakes. There is no grace in the process, but only fear.

There is no fear in love. But perfect love drives out fear, because fear has to do with punishment. The one who fears is not made perfect in love.
1 John 4:18, NIV

Discipline is a form of love. It's the feeling that God, or others, are actually looking out for your best interest and want to see you come forth into bridal maturity. Love is at the very heart of discipline.

My son, do not despise the Lord's discipline and do not resent his rebuke, because the Lord disciplines those he loves, as a father the son he delights in.
Proverbs 3:11–12, NIV

What caring parent would not discipline his son or daughter? They know their children better than anyone else does, and they know what is best for them. Parents are not just looking at mistakes when they discipline their children, but at the fruit and harvest they will reap in the future. If you are a parent and never discipline your children because you say you love them too much and don't want to hurt them, then let me say it lovingly, yet truthfully–you are not really loving them. It is only through loving discipline and correction that we can gain a heart of wisdom. That is where the child truly grows. Do you realize that if we hate correction, we are considered stupid and are said to despise ourselves?

> *Whoever loves discipline loves knowledge, but he who hates correction is stupid.*
>
> Proverbs 12:1, NIV

> *He who listens to a life–giving rebuke will be at home among the wise. He who ignores discipline despises himself, but whoever heeds correction gains understanding.*
>
> Proverbs 15:31–32, NIV

Let us read the classic passage in Hebrews 12 and get a better understanding of God's discipline as we are going to learn from the Shulamite in Song of Solomon 3.

> *In your struggle against sin, you have not yet resisted to the point of shedding your blood. And you have forgotten that word of encouragement that addresses you as sons: My son, do not make light of the Lord's discipline, and do not lose heart when he rebukes you, because the Lord disciplines those he loves, and he punishes everyone he accepts as a son. Endure hardship as discipline; God is treating you as sons. For what son is not disciplined by his father? If you are not disciplined (and everyone undergoes discipline), then you are illegitimate children and not true sons. Moreover, we have all had human fathers who disciplined us and we respected them for it. How much more should we submit to the Father of our spirits and live! Our fathers disciplined us for a little while as they thought best; but God disciplines us for our good, that we may share in his holiness. No discipline seems pleasant at the time, but painful. Later on, however, it produces a harvest of righteousness and peace for those who have been trained by it.*
>
> Hebrews 12:4–11, NIV

The Discipline of God

It is important to understand who the writer of Hebrews is addressing as he is talking about the discipline of God the Father. He is addressing sons! I just love it. Discipline is a proof of sonship. It proves that we are sons of God. Not only are we the Bride of Jesus, the Bridegroom God, but we are sons to the heavenly Father. It is our two–core identities. We are sons and we are the Bride (see Revelation 21:7, 9).

The very fact that we are disciplined by the Father is a proof of His great love for us. For many of us, that discipline can look different. Remember, the Shulamite is being disciplined because of her refusal to obey. Being disciplined by God means He is treating us as a loving Father, and not a hard task–master. He disciplines us for our ultimate good and for His ultimate pleasure. If we are not disciplined by God, then we are illegitimate sons. To be disciplined means that God deeply cares about us and has not given up on us; that He greatly longs for something in us and wants to bring us into our destiny. It is a terrible thing to get away with sin and compromise for a long time, because that means that God is giving up on us. But the fact that we come under chastisement is the proof of His great leadership over our lives. Instead of running away from God in fear, we will seek Him in love.

The Father is so merciful, gracious, slow to anger and rich in love. It's who He is forever! When He disciplines us, it's out of these four distinct pillars of His heart (see Psalm 103:8). He is committed to seeing us come up out of the wilderness, leaning upon our Beloved. He loves us too much to allow us to come up short of becoming His glorious sons, and a mature Bride for His Beloved Son. He feels the pain of those He disciplines and continues to consider them as His close friends. He hates the sin yet delights in the ones He disciplines. When we can't seem to figure out what God is doing in our lives, especially when were under His chastisement, we usually have a rejection mindset. We think that God is looking for a reason to eliminate us. We think He is playing with our minds and trying to make our lives difficult. We don't think He understands us. We don't think He desires to bless and favor us. But that is not the truth at all. When we're under discipline, we must learn how to catch the little foxes of lies and accusations that are trying to spoil the garden of our heart.

> *Catch us the foxes, The little foxes that spoil the vines, For our vines have tender grapes.*
> Song of Solomon 2:15

We often have a wrong concept of discipline and that is why so many of us believe lies about the nature of God's heart. Our thinking patterns are not in agreement with His. We must break off any negative judgments against God's perfect leadership. We must reject and renounce all the lies of the enemy that says, "God must be mad at me or disappointed with me. Maybe I have gone too far and He is now cutting me off. Maybe His patience has run out." Instead of giving into these lies, we must renounce and reject them and declare to heaven and hell that our Father is beautiful and kind, faithful and humble, fair and good and righteous and holy. Let us proclaim that all of His dealings in our lives are loving and faithful.

> *All the ways of the Lord are loving and faithful for those who keep the demands of his covenant.*
> Psalm 25:10, NIV

Before we peer into the Shulamite being disciplined in Song of Solomon 3, let's look at the heart and motive of why God disciplines His sons. This will help us now and in the future to be in total agreement with Jesus and not the enemy.

Why the Father Disciplines His Sons

Understanding why God disciplines us is very important. Let's take a further look at it. We will soon get back to the journey of the Shulamite in Song of Solomon 3. Keep in

The Discipline of God

mind, she is under discipline and does not feel the manifest presence of God in her life. She is upon her bed, reflecting what had just happened. It's very exciting to see how she responds to it, and what happens inside her heart. Knowing why God disciplines His chosen ones will help us to better understand the storyline in the Shulamite's life.

There are many reasons why the Father disciplines us. I want to give you a simple list and encourage you to go and develop these on your own. But after I give you this list, I want to delve back into Hebrews 12 and sum up all these reasons into one scriptural explanation for why God disciplines us. Here are reasons why the heavenly Father disciplines His sons:

- Because of His great love and mercy for us
- To remove any form of darkness in us and all that hinders love for Him
- To keep us humble and dependent upon Him
- To own us completely
- To demonstrate that we are the sons of God
- So we will not compromise anymore and take God for granted
- To prepare us for the marriage of the Lamb
- So we will not deny our faith and be condemned on the last day

Now let us look again at Hebrews 12.

Our fathers disciplined us for a little while as they thought best; but God disciplines us for our good, that we may share in his holiness. No discipline seems pleasant at the time, but painful. Later on, however, it produces a harvest of righteousness and peace for those who have been trained by it.
Hebrews 12:10–12, NIV

It is very clear from this text that the Father disciplines us as sons so we can be partakers of His holiness and produce a harvest of righteousness and peace. That's the primary purpose of discipline. The Father wants us to see His bright jasper glory upon His throne (see Revelation 4:3). He wants to take us up in the Spirit and consume us with the light and splendor of His majesty. He wants to be seen and known for who He is.

Hebrews 12 tells us that we cannot see God unless we are holy. He wants us to be just like Him in character. He longs for us to share and partner with Him in His holiness and transcendent pleasure. He knows that we have many hidden areas of darkness that need to be blotted out. He knows what it is that is keeping us from entering the holy of holies.

I just love the honesty of the writer of Hebrews, as he says that the process of discipline is very painful. But if we are trained by it (meaning, if we allow God to do whatever He wants in us and we gladly embrace it with perseverance), then we will reap a harvest of righteousness and peace. It will bring a radical change within our inner man, which is the most precious jewel to the heart of God. We will be the bright righteousness that Isaiah prophesied.

> *For Zion's sake I will not hold my peace, And for Jerusalem's sake I will not rest, Until her righteousness goes forth as brightness, And her salvation as a lamp that burns.*
>
> Isaiah 62:1

When we are under discipline from the heart of God, we must neither despise nor be discouraged by it. We are told not to make light of the situation nor lose heart during the process. There are two specific things that we cannot afford to neglect when were being trained in the wilderness. We must have a laser beam focus upon these two things: confidence and perseverance.

The Discipline of God

So do not throw away your confidence; it will be richly rewarded. You need to persevere so that when you have done the will of God, you will receive what he has promised.
Hebrews 10:35–36, NIV

If we lose our confidence while under the rod of the Lord, we lose our reward. If we don't have perseverance in times of testing, then we lose what God promised. If we remain confident in God's passionate love and commitment to us and persevere under His discipline, then we will receive a rich reward from heaven. Isn't that what your heart wants? Isn't that the very cry of your heart? Keep in mind that perseverance feeds on confidence. If you want to further study the subject of perseverance, then go the James 1 and let God give you divine revelation.

The Shulamite's Specific Discipline

Now let's get back to the Shulamite's journey in Song of Solomon 3. She was not willing to climb mountains and face adversity with her Beloved in Song of Solomon 2, so now she is paying the price. She went from delight in the daytime to pain in the night. She went from the apple tree to her own bed. Just listen to her confession:

By night on my bed I sought the one I love; I sought him, but I did not find him.
Song of Solomon 3:1

She could not find her Beloved! That was her biggest fear and her deepest pain. She was not supposed to be upon her bed, but up on the mountains of Bether with the Lord (2:17). The mountains of Bether means "the mountains of division." They were located east side of the Jordan valley. These mountains intersected with deep valleys, separating the Shulamite from the heavenly Bridegroom. Do you remember her bold statement that she made back in chapter 1? It was the cry that consumed her soul.

Draw me away! We will run after you. The king has brought me into his chambers. We will be glad and rejoice in you. We will remember your love more than wine. Rightly do they love you.

Song of Solomon 1:4

She declared that she was willing to be drawn in intimacy with her Beloved and was willing to run after Him in divine partnership. She would go wherever her Beloved wanted her to go. But obviously, she didn't follow through on her commitment in chapter 2. The Lord was requiring a new level of obedience in her. He wanted her to embrace the new assignment, which required a new measure of faith. He wanted to lift her vision higher! This definitely challenged her security. Who was she going to lean upon? Who was she going to surrender herself to? I believe she was more confident in herself than in His commitment to her.

As I already mentioned, it is important for us to understand that the Shulamite's painful compromise was rooted in fear and not rebellion. It was deep seated fear and broken trust that was never fully dealt with under the apple tree or in the King's chambers. Maybe you wonder what was she afraid of. What was her hidden fear? I believe she feared total obedience and total surrender in this prophetic season. She feared that one hundred percent obedience would be too difficult and costly for her. She feared taking new risks and leaving her comfort zone. She did not think that she had the strength to fully follow and obey the One she loved.

This is exactly where most of the body of Christ is living today in our present generation. There are so many of God's people who want to love God with all their heart and serve Him with all their strength, but when the Lord suddenly comes and challenges their comfort zone and requires new levels of dedication and radical abandonment, it seems that's where the line is truly drawn. But it's not enough to just say we really love God. It is not enough for us to tell our friends how willing we are to give up everything for His Name's sake. We must be willing to say yes to the heart of God when He challenges us and simply follow through. I am definitely speaking to myself.

I believe we need to have God give us a new paradigm of what His heart is like and the rewards that He desires to bestow upon those who say yes to one hundred percent obedience. God does reward and bless those who hunger and thirst after righteousness and obedience.

Blessed are those who hunger and thirst for righteousness, For they shall be filled.
Matthew 5:6

Up until this point, whenever the Shulamite sought after her Beloved and His affections for her, she discovered them. She hasn't ever been denied. She's gotten everything she asked and sought for. But now her time of discovery will be different. She will not get what she pursues at this specific time in her life. In (1:2), she discovered that Jesus' love was better than wine. In (1:3), she discovered that His Name is like perfume poured forth. In (1:4), she discovered the beauty and romance of the King. In (2:3), she tasted of Jesus' supreme pleasure. But now, in (3:1–5), things have changed.

We don't actually know how long the separation lasted. But we do know this for sure, that Jesus wanted her to dance upon the very things that terrified her up on the mountains! So what does her Beloved do about her refusal to this invitation?

God's Manifest Presence is Withdrawn

Jesus withdraws the one thing she loves most—His glorious presence. She experiences the discipline of God as He hides His face from her. The sweetness of Song of Solomon 2 is gone. The Lord is not angry with her, but He is jealous over her heart and wants her to be a mature Bride in deep partnership with Him. That's where He's taking her. The

Lord lifted His presence from her, in order to awaken fresh hunger and trust in her. He wanted her to have a new resolve in her devotion. She is still a Shulamite. He knows that she is not a false lover even though she feared to go to the mountains with Him. The very fact that God lifted His presence is a statement of His zeal and commitment to her and not His anger or wrath. He just turned up the heat to produce a deeper level of love, trust and obedience in her. It's His kindness to her! Let us keep in mind that when God does lift His manifest presence, He is not mad or angry. He is alerting us to the seriousness of our compromise. He is teaching us humility and meekness. He is awakening fresh hunger and dependence upon Him. That's why He lifts His presence!

God does the same with us that He did for the Shulamite. There are seasons when He withdraws His manifest presence from us when we simply refuse to obey and step out in faith. Is there anything more painful than not finding the One we love? The pain of absence: is the Lord playing hard-to-get or teaching us not to take Him for granted?

God withdraws His manifest presence, not to shut our hearts down, but to awaken love for Him. This is exactly what He was doing with the Shulamite. Let's read the verse again in Song of Solomon 3 and see what is happening in her heart.

> *By night on my bed I sought the one I love; I sought him, but I did not find him.*
>
> *Song of Solomon 3:1*

Do you notice that it's at night when this is taking place? In the Hebrew text, by night literally means "by nights." It's plural and not singular. It is referring to one night after another. I believe we can relate to this. How many times have you found yourself saying, "How long until this trial ends?" It seems like it will never end. It seems like one night turns into two nights and two nights turns into two hundred nights. Isn't that right?

The Discipline of God

It was St. John of the Cross who came up with the phrase "The dark night of the soul." This is the very first time the Shulamite experiences the dark night of her soul. And this will not be the last for her, as she will face it again in chapter 5 in a much deeper way. The Lord is so tender and gracious to her; He's preparing her for the biggest test of her life. But we will get to that later.

Seeking the One She Loves

It is night, so she is naturally upon her bed. It's more than a place of comfort; it is a place where she can be totally vulnerable and transparent; it's a place where she can let down the hidden walls of her heart and can seek the One her heart loves. The Shulamite was not doing a new thing when she is seeking God upon her bed. King David did the same thing. Listen to what he says:

> *Be angry, and do not sin. Meditate within your heart on your bed, and be still. Selah!*
>
> Psalm 4:4

> *When I remember You on my bed, I meditate on You in the night watches.*
>
> Psalm 63:6

Even though she cannot find Him, she is pictured meditating upon her bed and *reflecting* where she went wrong. She is a lover of God and wants to learn the ways of God in her life. As she reflects in the night time, she is about to take her love and devotion to a whole new level. Her time of reflection upon her bed is going to pay off.

She fully realizes how she refused to simply obey and ascend unto the mountains and that is what caused this time of separation. So now she arises from her bed and goes out in the city and streets to look for Her Beloved. Just listen to her fervent cry!

> *"I will arise now," I said, "And go about the city; in the streets and in the squares I will seek the one I love." I sought him, but I did not find him.*
>
> Song of Solomon 3:2

I just love the language of the Shulamite's heart as she is seeking her Beloved in the city of Jerusalem, boldly declaring, "I will seek the one I love." The Hebrew word for "seek" is *baqash*. It means to seek to find, to desire, to seek the face, to explore and to encounter. It speaks of an ardent repetition that denotes perseverance. This is what she is doing, even though she is under discipline. She still has a seeking heart like when she first attracted His gaze (2:9). She refuses to give up. She desires to explore her Beloved and receive a breakthrough in her spirit. The word can also be applied to the breaking in of day. She wants to come out of her time of discipline just like the breaking in of the day. She is a lover of God.

She is now out of her house and is in the city of Jerusalem, among the streets and squares where people interact. This is a place of risk, conflict and danger. She thought the mountains would be dangerous, but little did she know where she would end up. The city is so much different from the apple tree and the King's chambers. It is a place where she feels vulnerable, but because of her love for Him, the risk is worth it!

What an encouragement for us. We don't have to throw in the towel or be offended when we're under discipline. We can be seeking to encounter the One our heart loves while under chastisement, just like the Shulamite. Let's pause here for a moment and take a deep breath!

Now it's important to know that as she sought after her Beloved, she did not find Him immediately. Remember, this was a new experience for her. All through chapters 1 and 2, when she sought Him she found Him. But this is a different and wonderful season for her in which she will receive

The Discipline of God

a deeper revelation of the heart of her Beloved! What I love about her response is her persistence to run *after* Him and not run *away* from Him. She could easily be offended by Him as He withdraws His manifest presence from her. She could say that it wouldn't be worth it to seek after Him; what if He let her down and she gets more hurt? But this is not the case for this woman who is being prepared to be a Bride. Even though she feared going to the mountains, she doesn't fear going downtown Jerusalem to search for her Beloved. The fact that she's fervently seeking after Him reveals this.

The pain of losing His presence motivates her to arise off her bed and seek the One her heart loves. She understands that prayer alone will not solve her problem. It requires active obedience. She must put feet to her prayers. Her soul is now becoming desperate. Her cry is strongly emerging within to find Him. We see the same response in David's heart when his heart felt distant from God.

> *O God, You are my God; Early will I seek you; My soul thirsts for you; My flesh longs for you in a dry and thirsty land where there is no water. So I have looked for you in the sanctuary, To see your power and your glory.*
>
> Psalm 63:1–2

We may be impressed with the Shulamite seeking the One she loves while not feeling the presence of the Lord. But the basic question we must ask ourselves is this: are we seeking the One we say we love? Are we still crying out to Him for the breaking in of the day, even while under discipline? Seeking is all about love! It's what separates servants from friends, slaves from sons and workers from lovers. There are many people who are seeking God, but what are they seeking after? You would be amazed at the hidden motives of why we are seeking God. We can be seeking God for ministry, position, influence, power or wealth. But there is something so much greater and awesome than these small things. The One who is love desires to be sought after and will not force Himself on anyone. He is looking and searching for voluntary lovers who only want Him and Him alone. He desires to be enough for us (see Psalm 73:25). Let us line back up with heaven and let our seeking after God's heart be only about love (see 1 John 5:3).

The Shulamite's love and devotion is increasing as she is getting to the point of desperation. It seems like she is about to have a breakthrough with the fervency she is showing, as she's seeking her Beloved with all of her heart. But we must understand that her time of discipline is not over. Even though she is seeking hard after Him, she still cannot find Him. She mentions this twice.

> *By night on my bed I sought the one I love; I sought him, but I did not find him. "I will arise now," I said, "And go about the city; in the streets and in the squares I will seek the one I love." I sought him, but I did not find him.*
>
> Song of Solomon 3:1-2

How frustrating it is when you are pouring out your soul and seeking God with all your strength and you can't seem to find your Beloved. It seems as though the heavens are brass, as though you just lost the pearl of great price. I believe we can all relate to the journey of the Shulamite in this season. But let's keep this thought in mind when nothing seems to be working: it's the impossibilities that produce a groan, a groan produces a voice, and a voice produces destiny!

The Shulamite said no to the mountains, but she said yes to seek after Jesus on her bed and in the streets of Jerusalem. The Lord was being very patient with her by giving her much time to say yes to the mountains. He won't force Her because it goes against the nature of His heart. But He will keep affirming who she is to Him and He will affirm who He is to her. It's just a matter of time before she has the confidence to go up to the mountains. Jesus was content with her in the streets for now, but He will come back and invite her again to go to the mountains with Him. Because He is a conquering King, He wants her to become a conquering Bride!

The Watchmen

As the Shulamite seeks her Beloved in the streets, she runs into the watchmen.

> *The watchmen who go about the city found me; "Have you seen the one I love?"*
> Song of Solomon 3:3

Remember, there are two types of watchmen in Song of Solomon. There are the "David watchmen" which we see here in chapter 3. And there are the "Saul watchmen" in chapter 5. Let us take a minute and understand what their role is.

Historically, they were city guards who went about the city for the preservation of its peace and safety. They were responsible to oversee the affairs of Jerusalem. Allegorically, the watchmen are the elders of the church. They are the spiritual leaders who exercised authority over God's people.

While the Shulamite paces up and down the streets searching for her Beloved, she probably got restless within her soul. She had been up all night, but still could not find Him. How frustrating! She might be thinking to herself, "How long will it be until I find the One I love? How many more long nights must my soul wrestle through?" But suddenly, when she least expects it, the watchmen find her downtown as they are making their rounds in the city. They noticed that she was deeply troubled inside her heart. So they desire to help her.

Once the Shulamite runs into the watchmen, she asks if they have any news of her Beloved. She says, "Have you seen the one I love?" (3:3). She is inflamed with love! She is a lover of God. She is a woman of the heart. She has a holy resolution to find her Beloved and is unwilling to settle for anything less.

Why do I call these watchmen the David watchmen? It is because they are so willing to help the Shulamite find her Beloved. They want her to reach her highest calling in God's heart. They are not threatened by her zeal but are motivated to see her soaring in her heart with her Lover. They are pushing her closer rather than pulling her away from God's heart. They definitely have the heart of David as spiritual leaders. They help her find Him. That's the great mark of leadership!

The Shulamite exclaims in a rapture of joy, "I found the one my heart loves!" There is nothing else that she desires in her pilgrimage while on the earth. She found Him. She never gave up and kept pressing in until she found the pearl of great price. The sweet presence that she experienced in chapter 2 has now returned. Praise God!

Jesus' Manifest Presence Returns

The Lord suddenly crashes in like a tidal wave and reveals His glorious presence to her in response to her love, devotion and obedience. He was found by her in the streets of Jerusalem. He honors and rewards her seeking heart. Remember, this is your story and journey that you are discovering. This is the cry of your heart!

> *Scarcely had I passed by them, When I found the one I love. I held him and would not let him go, Until I had brought him to the house of my mother, And into the chamber of her who conceived me.*
> Song of Solomon 3:4

Once she finds her Beloved, she testifies that she will not let Him go (3:4). Imagine a weeping child who was lost, but now holds on to his mother; imagine the prodigal Father who

The Discipline of God

embraces His precious son who just returned home (see Luke 15:20). This is what is happening with the Shulamite and her Beloved. They are rejoicing in the deep connection they both had in the King's chambers and under the apple tree.

She now has a new resolution to hold on to Jesus and it came from her time of discipline. She is reaping a harvest of righteousness. She was well trained in the night hours, and her time of pain and correction produced a holy violence within her. She has an unquenchable determination to do the will of her Beloved as she prayed for in Song of Solomon 1:4. She is learning priceless lessons in her prophetic journey. Throughout the remainder of the song she never let's go of Him.

When the Shulamite finds her Beloved, she takes Him to the house of her mother.

> *Scarcely had I passed them when I found him whom my soul loves. I held him, and would not let him go until I had brought him into my mother's house; and into the chamber of her who conceived me.*
> Song of Solomon 3:4

The mother in Scripture refers to the Church. In Matthew 12:46–50, we are told that anyone who does the will of God is Jesus' mother and brother. Why was the Shulamite so concerned about bringing her Beloved into the chamber of Him who conceived her? Do you notice that she said she would not let Him go until He was inside the chamber? There are probably many reasons why she is so focused on this. But my guess is that she is not content to just have her Beloved for herself, but wants others in the Church to have Him as well. She is thinking of the interests of others (see Philippians 2:4). She is growing up and becoming less selfish. She is well on her way to becoming a Bride. She's reaping a harvest of righteousness from her time of discipline. She not only finds Him after a long time of discipline, but she brings Him to a place where others can learn the lessons of His heart.

Final Thoughts about God's Discipline

If we want to reap a harvest of righteousness and peace, and if we are to become a mature Bride in the eyes of heaven, then we must learn to submit to the heart of the Father when were under the rod of His discipline. Submission is a huge part of sonship. Just as Jesus submitted to His Father, so must we (see John 5:19). Just as Jesus learned obedience through the things which He suffered, so must we (see Hebrews 5:8).

When we submit to the Father, we are submitting to Him as the "Father of our spirits." The Father is the one who owns our soul. He wants to have us as a dwelling place for Himself. He deserves it. When we do submit under the discipline of God, guess what happens? Life!

> *...How much more should we submit to the Father of our spirits and live!*
> Hebrews 12:9, NIV

We can learn the same lesson the Shulamite learned on her journey; if she can embrace a season of discipline and have holy violence to go hard after God's heart, then so can we. If she can have a seeking heart in the night hours, then so can we. Instead of accusing God of being unfair, let's do what the Shulamite did in the dark night of her soul. Let's seek the One our hearts love and adore. Amen!

As we move into Song of Solomon 4, we see that the Shulamite receives a fresh revelation of who she is to her Beloved. You will find this beautiful back–and–forth dialogue between the Bridegroom and the Shulamite. Neither can stop boasting about who they are in the other's eyes. Listen to what Jesus has to say about the Shulamite after her season of discipline:

> *Behold, you are fair, my love! Behold, you are fair! You*

The Discipline of God

have dove's eyes behind your veil. Your hair is like a flock of goats, Going down from Mount Gilead. Your teeth are like a flock of shorn sheep which have come up from the washing, every one of which bears twins, And none is barren among them. Your lips are like a strand of scarlet, and your mouth is lovely. Your temples behind your veil Are like a piece of pomegranate. Your neck is like the tower of David, Built for an armory, On which hang a thousand bucklers, All shields of mighty men. Your two breasts are like two fawns, Twins of a gazelle, Which feed among the lilies.

Song of Solomon 4:1–5

In this passage of Scripture, Jesus uses the natural parts of the human body to convey a spiritual truth. Each concept is massive in its implication. Jesus praises several attributes of her beauty, but her eyes are what I want to focus on. The Lord is breaking out in great praise with a big smile over her. He simply cannot hold it in. He mentions how focused and meek she is becoming. Her devotion and gaze have increased. In Song of Solomon 1:15, Jesus praised her for having doves eyes. But here in Song of Solomon 4:1, He praises her for her meekness. He says, "You have dove's eyes behind your veil." Her gaze is hidden from man, just as the eyes of one who wears a veil is hidden from others. That means that the people in the city of Jerusalem could not really see how much she loved this Man from Nazareth. It was hidden from the common crowd. Her eyes behind her veil were precious and holy to His heart. They were eyes of love fully reserved for Her Beloved. The Shulamite is becoming a beautiful pearl–standing on the seashore of divine love! See appendix for further reading and recommended resources on Song of Solomon 4:1–5.

Now we are going to see a radical change take place in the heart of the Shulamite, regarding her decision to go to the mountains with her Beloved. Up until this time in her journey, she has said no to go to the mountains, but now she is going to say yes, not out of obligation, but of her own free will. We will soon discover the vast change and growth within her heart.

Questions to Ponder

1. When you are under discipline, do you feel like you are being loved by God or you're being picked on? Why?
2. When you feel that God has lifted His manifest presence from you, what is your attitude like and what do you do about it?
3. What fruit has God's discipline produced in your own life? Can you or others clearly identify it?

CHAPTER SEVEN

The Ravished Bridegroom God

Until the day breaks and the shadows flee away, I will go my way to the mountain of myrrh and to the hill of frankincense. You are all fair, my love, and there is no spot in you. Come with me from Lebanon, my spouse, with me from Lebanon. Look from the top of Amana, from the top of Senir and Hermon, from the lions' dens, from the mountains of the leopards. You have ravished my heart, My sister, my spouse; You have ravished my heart with one look of your eyes, With one link of your necklace. How fair is your love, my sister, my spouse! How much better than wine is your love, and the scent of your perfumes than all spices!
Song of Solomon 4:6–10

After a season of divine discipline and affirmation from the Beloved, the Shulamite is now willing to go to the mountains. Jesus now surprises her by telling her how He feels toward her inside His heart. It is one of the most stunning revelations of His heart. It's one of the key passages and grand themes in the Song of Solomon. Jesus speaks with such boldness yet tenderly and says, "you have ravished my heart, my sister, my spouse" (4:9). He not only says it once, but He says it twice. The heart of God was ravished over this simple farm girl.

We must remember that the Shulamite is not yet fully mature in love. She is still weak and has not fully become Jesus' inheritance yet, but she is on her way. She is definitely learning to give herself in wholehearted surrender to Jesus' Lordship.

What motivates Jesus to speak this incredible revelation over her? What is it that strikes a chord within His heart to make Him speak such a powerful truth of being ravished over her in this season of her journey? I believe it is the Shulamite's fearless and wholehearted commitment to say yes to her Beloved to go her way to the mountain of myrrh with Him. It is her willingness that ravishes His heart. Remember, she was invited to go to the mountains in chapter 2, but she refused because of fear. But now she has come to a place in her walk with her Beloved where she is willing to leave her comfort zone. She is willing to go to the place that terrified her. The place that she feared the most will become the place that she dances upon with her Beloved.

The Shulamite Goes Her Way to the Mountain

Let us listen to the Shulamite's awesome willingness to ascend the mountain with the One she is in love with. Let's hear from her own soul the cry that moved and ravished the heart of God. As I mentioned in the introduction, this is the very turning point in the song for the Shulamite.

> *Until the day breaks and the shadows flee away, I will go my way to the mountain of myrrh and to the hill of frankincense.*
>
> Song of Solomon 4:6

Do you notice that she says that she will go "my way" to the mountain of myrrh? It is not someone else's way nor is it her pastor's way, but it is her own way that she says yes to. She agrees to deeply embrace the Cross. She no longer fears one hundred percent obedience. She is willing to embrace the challenge of leaving her comfort zone from Song of Solomon 2. A radical change has now taken place in her heart. She is willing to face any enemy of her soul up on the mountains with her Beloved.

> *Come with me from Lebanon, my spouse, With me from Lebanon. Look from the top of Amana, From the top of Senir and Hermon, From the lions' dens, From the mountains of the leopards.*
>
> Song of Solomon 4:8

She did it! She's overcome a hidden fear that was tucked away inside her heart and is now willing to follow her Beloved at any cost. Jesus was so tender with her, because in Song of Solomon 2, He did not tell her about all of the dangers that were on the mountains, including lions and leopards, but after she says yes in 4:6, He then lets her know about what really lies ahead. Let us take a peek at these mountains mentioned in Song of Solomon 4:8.

- Lebanon–It was an invitation for her to leave the mountains bordering between the hostile lands north of Palestine and the Promised Land.
- Amana–It was in the south near Damascus.
- Senir (also called Hermon)–It was a sacred mountain twenty miles long with three peaks.

These are the mountains the Shulamite is about to conquer. Jesus doesn't just want her up among these mountains, but He wants her at the top of them, looking down. He wants her to be a conqueror. That is His burning jealousy. Now it's important to understand that the she doesn't literally go up to these mountains until Song of Solomon 5 where she will ultimately face the most difficult season in her journey. But Jesus, the Beloved, sees the sincere cry within her heart and sees her willing spirit to obey Him and do His will. He sees the longing of her soul to fully love Him, even though she doesn't fully understand what He's trying to produce in her. This is your story!

What was it that helped motivate the Shulamite to say yes to go to the mountains? It didn't just happen by accident. She refused before, but now she's willing. I am sure there were a lot of deep things taking place inside her that we don't fully understand. But there is one thing that clearly sticks out to me. It's the *constant affirmation* of Jesus' affections over her. Affirmation is what helped equip her to say yes to face any obstacle in her life, including deep, hidden fear. Jesus is her best cheerleader. He believes in her like no one else does. He keeps saying to her, "Come on, I know you can do it. You are a champion in my sight. Yes, you're a champion because a champion lives in you." Now obviously this is not the exact language written in the Song of Solomon, but it's the essence of what He is communicating over her. Let's take a look at a few verses in chapter 4 and see how the Lord strategically grabs hold of her and produces a confidence in her without violating her free will.

> *How beautiful you are, my darling! Oh how beautiful! Your eyes behind your veil are doves...*
> Song of Solomon 4:1, NIV

> *Your neck is like the tower of David, built with elegance; on it hang a thousand shields, all of them shields of warriors.*
> Song of Solomon 4:4, NIV

Jesus first declares that she has dove's eyes and they are behind her veil (4:1). Remember, we just looked at them in the last chapter. Jesus also tells her that her neck, which speaks of her will, is like the tower of David (4:4). The tower of David is an ancient citadel located near the Jaffa gate entrance to the old city of Jerusalem. It was built to strengthen a strategically weak point in the old city's defenses. Jesus is telling her that her will is becoming strong and very *willing* to Him. It's probable that this verse just rocked her world. Maybe she was always told how rebellious she was. Maybe

The Ravished Bridegroom God

she didn't think she had a willing spirit. Maybe she never thought she could become so dedicated in her walk with her Beloved. But that's the point! Jesus sees her so differently than the common eye. He sees the deep cry and stirrings in her heart to be a lover of God. He told her that she was willing. When He says that her neck is like the tower of David, He's letting her know how strong her cry and willing spirit is. The neck is directly related to the will. If you decide to turn your neck to the left, then you will go that way. If you decide to turn your neck to the right, then you will go that way. So basically said: Jesus looked at her in the eyes and spoke to her heart and said, "You're willing." He probably kept hitting this over and over, until she was convinced herself. It wasn't about her trying to convince her Beloved how dedicated she was, but it was about Him convincing her how dedicated *He* was to *her*. That's a huge difference.

It was the Shulamite's will (her sincere cry and determination) that was worth more than anything else to her Beloved that ravished His heart. A willing spirit is what He has been producing in her. What an amazing testimony. Jesus says that her will is just like the tower of David, built with elegance.

She made the ultimate confession: "I'm willing. I will go my way." There are no pockets of resistance within her. She is now more in the relationship for Him than for herself. She's growing up. God is beginning to take ownership of her. She is on her way to mature love.

Let us soak in the text again and allow it to become something very precious to us on our journey with our Beloved, just like the Shulamite.

> *Until the day breaks and the shadows flee away, I will go my way to the mountain of myrrh and to the hill of frankincense.*
> Song of Solomon 4:6

I believe this is the very cry of your heart. You have had some deep struggles and fears that have kept you from going your way to the mountain of myrrh, but now you are in a season with the Lord where you are willing to do the very thing you struggle with. This can mean so many different things for each one of you. Only you and God know what that is. But you are not going to allow a spirit of fear to keep you from fulfilling your destiny. You're willing just like the Shulamite. You will ravish the heart of the Bridegroom. Amen!

The Shulamite uses *two distinct words* in her confession to go to the mountains: "myrrh" and "frankincense." She calls it the mountain of myrrh and the hill of frankincense. Let us take a look at them and get a better understanding of what she is trying to communicate.

Myrrh is a burial spice that is very costly, and it has a great and wonderful fragrance. In Scripture, myrrh speaks of Jesus' death. In application, it speaks of dying to self. It is a burial spice to our flesh, but it's a fragrance to our spirit. We must embrace our way (which is ultimately God's way) to the mountain of myrrh and refuse to comfort the flesh. It is a mountain and not a small hill that we must conquer. That mountain is a specific challenge for each of us. It takes time and effort to climb a mountain. Just as Jesus ascended the mountain of myrrh in His own life when He went to the Cross, so must we. There is no other way. We must take up our cross daily and deny ourselves, so we can ascend the mountains with our Beloved!

> *Then he said to them all, "If anyone desires to come after Me, let him deny himself, and take up his cross daily, and follow Me. For whoever desires to save his life will lose it, but whoever loses his life for My sake will save it."*
>
> Luke 9:23–24

The Ravished Bridegroom God

Frankincense, or incense, throughout Scripture speaks of prayer and intercession. It is something very sweet and glorious to the heart of God. It has an incredible smell and aroma. We ascend the hill of frankincense to receive strength to ascend the mountain of myrrh. Jesus exhorted Peter to pray to receive the strength he needed to face temptation (see Matthew 26:40–41). The mountain of myrrh is too difficult to ascend without living on the hill of frankincense. Our prayer life empowers our hearts to embrace the Cross with self–denial. We can only embrace the mountain of myrrh (self denial) to the measure that we go up to the hill of frankincense (intercession). This is our way forward to live and abide under Jesus' Lordship!

We Must Go Our Way to the Mountain

May we learn to say yes to the heart of Jesus' and go our way to the mountain of myrrh with Him, just like the Shulamite did. She set a great example for us to follow, even though she refused the first time. She was revealing to us that no matter what the cost is He is worth it all. No matter how painful it is, He is so beautiful. He deserves the reward of His just sufferings! How glorious these words are to God: "I will go my way." We must follow the unique path God has chosen for us. God calls each of us on our own tailor–made journey. His way of training each one of us is unique. That is why it's very important that we don't try and compare ourselves with anyone else.

The heavenly Bridegroom has wisely chosen our way for us, and it's perfect. There are absolutely no mistakes in His plan. His wisdom is unlimited (see Romans 11:33). God has laid out our individual seasons to bring us into wholehearted love. He knows exactly what He is doing and does whatever He pleases (see Daniel 4:35). He is the master potter. We must go our way because it's the only way. No one else can take it for us. He wants us to embrace our own special way of the wilderness. He has carefully marked out all the days of our lives and wants His way to be our way and our way to be His way.

It's important that we are jealous over our way and press into it with zeal and vigor. We must understand the journey that God has for us, so we can stand against the accusations of the enemy. Knowing our way is the word of our testimony that will overcome the enemy's tactics (see Revelation 12:11).

If you are really having a hard time and struggle to surrender your will to God, then I want to encourage you to go meditate and pray Philippians 2 on a regular basis. Paul the Apostle gives a distinct key for those who are struggling within their will. It's a very practical and powerful revelation.

> *For it is God who works in you to will and to act according to his good pleasure.*
> Philippians 2:13, NIV

Paul focuses completely upon the will that doesn't want to surrender or bow. He tells us the solution and the way forward. He says that it is God Himself who works within us and does it according to His own good pleasure. Only He has the ability to work within our own will and change it. What He is accomplishing is only good, but we need to cooperate with Him and be willing. We must continually pray and cry out for God to work in us until we are willing to do the very thing that's holding us down. This is a passage that I keep hitting over and over in my personal life, so I will be very willing to go my way to the mountain of myrrh. It helps break the stubbornness in my life. To say no to God's will is more costly than saying yes.

Before we begin to look at the ravished Bridegroom God in Song of Solomon 4:9, I want to share my own personal struggle with my unwillingness to fully surrender myself to the heart and purposes of God. Just as it took some time for the Shulamite to embrace her mountain, so it has taken me some time to embrace my mountain. And it's still a process in my journey!

As I look back over my walk with God, there have been many things I have struggled with. Some of them I have already conquered by the grace of God. But there are still many pockets of resistance within my soul to the ways and purposes of God. My biggest battle has not been with the devil; nor has it been with humans, although I have always thought that other people were the source of my problems. I found myself always blaming them—it took responsibility off of me for my own actions. But other people were not my problem. The biggest problem and struggle I have faced is myself. I am my biggest problem, period. I call it the clashing of two wills. It's *my* will versus *God's* will. My will is more focused on myself and what I can get. It's serving God on my terms, just like the Shulamite did in the first four chapters of Song of Solomon. The reason why I couldn't fully yield myself to God's will is because of the wrong image that I had of Him; I doubted His goodness for me personally. I didn't believe that the will of God was absolutely perfect for me (see Romans 12:2). I feared that somehow He was going to make my life and circumstances very difficult, or I feared that He would let me down when the pressure intensified. I was afraid to give Him full control, because it made me feel very vulnerable. I was not willing to serve God on His terms without having all the answers or solutions in my life. But I now realize that I must submit to God's purposes even when everything within me wants to resist. I must trust His heart and know that it's His goodness and mercy that's going to follow me and chase me down.

> *Surely goodness and mercy shall follow me all the days of my life; and I will dwell in the house of the Lord forever.*
>
> Psalm 23:6

The Father in heaven has chosen a unique path for my

prophetic journey. It has been well thought through in His mind. Even though I know that He desires and plans what is best for me, I have still struggled to embrace and surrender my will to His will, living and abiding under Jesus' Lordship. So what has been God's will for me in this season of my life? What is the mountain that I have to climb and conquer? The mountain of myrrh for me is related to the issue of *embracing nothingness*. To embrace nothingness means that I have absolutely nothing to hold or cling to but God Himself. It means I cannot hold on to my ministry, my position, my leadership, my reputation or my future destiny, which I'm always trying to do. God has purposely withheld the very things I desire, in order to bring me to a place where I have nothing in my life but Jesus Himself. Now that doesn't mean that it's wrong to have any of these things. But holding on to these things has caused me to slowly drift away from loving God with all my heart and all my strength. Not having anything to hold on to but Jesus has been my mountain of myrrh. I have been fighting it so long, because it makes me feel very vulnerable, and when I see other leaders who have a position in ministry and are flourishing in it, it really makes the whole process even more difficult. This just reveals the brokenness in my identity. But by the grace of God, I am now choosing to embrace my own mountain and trust God's perfect leadership over my life. I am coming to a place where I understand that ministry, position and leadership will all one day fade away. Everyone and everything will change, but God will never change. He is far more beautiful and glorious than anything this world has to offer. His greatness is now my pursuit, and the mountain that once seemed so huge to me, is beginning to melt before His surpassing greatness!

> *Behold, God is great, and we do not know Him; nor can the number of His years be discovered.*
>
> Job 36:26

I do want to make clear that it's not wrong to contend for

leadership position and ministry. God wants to give us the desires of our hearts (see Psalm 37:4). But we must search out the hidden motives of what or who we are really chasing after. We must discover what brings the greatest pleasure inside of us; Jesus Himself or position in ministry. I now understand the difference between contending and demanding. I contend for the dreams in my heart, but I don't slip into demanding from God. It is by the grace of God that I am slowly beginning to learn this valuable lesson of surrendering my demands, and letting Jesus be my great role model in life. The One who made Himself nothing owes me nothing!

> *Who, being in very nature God, did not consider equality with God something to be grasped, but made himself nothing, taking the very nature of a servant, being made in human likeness. And being found in appearance as a man, he humbled himself and became obedient to death—even death on a cross! Therefore God exalted him to the highest place and gave him the name that is above every name.*
>
> Philippians 2:6–9, NIV

Jesus did not cling to His rights as God. He emptied Himself. Now that doesn't mean that He gave up His Deity, but He laid aside His glory (see John 17:5). He didn't hold on to His position or reputation, but humbled Himself and took upon the very nature of a servant. He didn't demand anything from His Father. It is a stunning love relationship they have. He was willing to let it go and had no desire to prove Himself. He was willing to embrace nothingness. Do you know why He is so beautiful? It's because He didn't want anything, but desired for the Father to have it all. His heart was broken for love and has never changed. Just as He didn't want to be seen as important or famous in the eyes of men in His first coming, so He will do the same thing when He turns everything over to His Father, after His millennial reign upon the earth.

> *Then comes the end, when He delivers the kingdom to God the Father, when He puts an end to all rule and all authority and power.*
>
> 1 Corinthians 15:24

Doesn't Jesus impress you? There is absolutely no heart like His. He lived a life of surrender. Just as He prayed in the garden for His Father's will and not His (see Matthew 26:39), so we must tread the same path and journey. Just as Jesus has a story to tell, so we will have one to tell also. In fact, Jesus Himself tells us that He who does the will of God to the end will have authority over the nations of the earth in the next age (see Revelation 2:26). This is what the journey of the Shulamite is teaching us. She shows us the wisdom of doing God's perfect will by saying yes to ascend to the mountains with our Beloved. He has destined us for greatness!

I believe there are two key questions we must ask ourselves concerning the battle of doing our will verses doing God's will. Now don't just think you automatically know the answer. Take some time and ponder them. Reflect back over your life and ask the Holy Spirit to confirm it. Ask Him if it's true or not?

1. Whose will are you chasing after? (see Luke 22:42).
2. Will you drink the Father's cup? (see John 18:11).

You would be amazed at how much of our emotional energy is consumed with doing our will rather than God's will, even though we *say* we will do His will. You would be amazed at how much of a war goes on inside our soul to drink the cup. We all have a cup to drink. We all have a mountain to climb and conquer. We all are being beckoned by God to do His perfect will to the very end. Why do we fight to do God's will? Here is just a simple list to think about:

- We don't personally believe God's goodness for us

The Ravished Bridegroom God

and have a wrong image of Him.
- We fear it's too difficult and are unwilling to give up our present lifestyle.
- We hate having nothing to hold on to that makes us feel important.
- We don't want to live in weakness and desire to have control.
- We don't want to live by faith and believe our way is better.
- We think that God wants to make our lives absolutely miserable.
- We don't like living in mystery and adventure.
- We don't like to embrace pain and adversity.
- We want immediate promotion and recognition.
- We don't look to the future rewards.
- We have not fully seen and discovered the beauty of God in a personal way.

We need to repent for fighting the perfect will of God in our lives. We need to repent for being unwilling to go our own way to the mountain of myrrh. We need to repent for trying to figure out God's will in our lives, as we always ask the question, "why?" Whenever we ask the question, why, we are not accepting the cup from the Father's heart. There is still a clashing going on between two wills. When we ask the question why in our circumstances, it only takes us to a place where we are not equipped to go. The book of Proverbs tells us that we are not to lean to our own understanding and reasoning.

> *Trust in the Lord with all your heart, And lean not on your own understanding; In all your ways acknowledge Him, And He shall direct your paths.*
> Proverbs 3:5–6

The most important thing for us on our journey to surrender to God's will is not to have all the information and details concerning our future, but to have the peace of God ruling and reigning upon the throne of our hearts. It's a peace that surpasses and transcends all understanding (see Philippians 4:7). I believe it's important to learn to separate our own understanding from God's own understanding. Our understanding wants every fact and minute detail. God's understanding wants us to trust Him without having all the facts and to live by faith. It might not make sense at first, but in due time, it will become more clear than ever. It will shine like the light of the morning.

We must learn to surrender our rights and demands. I remember Jack Frost, the founder of Shiloh Place Ministries, would always say that whatever we demand we will never inherit. I have found this to be very true. The very thing my soul wants most will just slip out of my hands if I insist on and demand it. We must let go and live a surrendered life. The only thing we can and must hold on to is King Jesus!

> *But whatever was to my profit I now consider loss for the sake of Christ. What is more, I consider everything a loss compared to the surpassing greatness of knowing Christ Jesus my Lord, for whose sake I have lost all things. I consider them rubbish, that I may gain Christ.*
> Philippians 3:7–8, NIV

Let us say yes to embracing the Cross (see Isaiah 53). Let us give God permission to shatter our self–will. Let us pray and ask God to usher us into His perfect will (see Hebrews 10:7). Let us bow to the purposes and ways of the Lord. It is so freeing to live a life of surrender, where Jesus is all in all. It won't be easy, but we can do it. The simple lesson I am learning about the wilderness and submitting to His will is this: it will either make you or break you. We either embrace the season in the wilderness or we fight it. The choice is up

The Ravished Bridegroom God

to us.

Well, I know we took a lot of time looking at the battle and struggle of surrendering our will and going our own way to the mountain of myrrh, but it was very important to look at. It's most likely the one thing the Holy Spirit is specifically highlighting. Without surrendering our will to the Lord, we can't grow into maturity and become a Bride; we remain as a Shulamite!

Let us get back to the journey of the Shulamite in Song of Solomon 4. So what was the response of Jesus, the Bridegroom God, to her willingness to say yes to go her own way to the mountain of myrrh? How did He feel inside His heart when this simple farm girl said the words, "I'm willing?" Let us read the passage again and feel the raging streams in Jesus' heart over her life.

> *You have ravished my heart, My sister, my spouse;*
> *You have ravished my heart with one look of your eyes,*
> *With one link of your necklace.*
> Song of Solomon 4:9

The Ravished Bridegroom God

What a prophetic declaration! Jesus has a ravished heart. This was His response to the Shulamite's fearless commitment to do His will. The God of all power, wealth and authority has a heart that is deeply moved and impacted. He is determined that she not miss the divine opportunity to experience His burning passion for her. He wants her to feel exactly how He feels over her as she says yes to His will and His purposes. He really cares and wants her to get it. He knows it will help equip and empower her heart for the future. Do you notice that He calls her "My sister" and "My spouse."

The NIV uses the word "bride" instead of spouse. This is the first time in the Song of Solomon that it is mentioned.

The Hebrew word for bride is *kallah*. It means to pierce through and carries the meaning of that which is brought to completion. This is what Jesus is doing in her heart. He is completing her. The Shulamite is walking into her ultimate destiny to be Jesus' Bride, ruling and reigning with Him forever.

Let us look at what the word ravished means. The Hebrew word for "ravished" is *labab*. It literally means "you have seized my heart." It means to be emotionally overcome with joy and delight. It means to be unusually attractive, pleasing or striking. Jesus was emotionally overcome with such radiant joy with the Shulamite, even in her weakness. Remember, she is still not yet a Bride, but He is still overcome by her. Her cry to love Him and obey Him moved and ravished His heart. He is smiling!

The ravished heart of God has a raging river of affections surging within His being. He is relentless in His pursuit of us. The very same way He felt over the life of the Shulamite is the exact way He feels about us when we choose to say yes to Him, even when we don't feel like it or it doesn't make sense. Not even the angels or the seraphim have the capacity to ravish God's heart, but we do! Doesn't that amaze you? Do you really understand who you are? Do you realize that the simple yet sincere cry in your spirit has more power to touch God's heart than the seraphim before His throne, and more than all the kings and armies of the earth? Why don't you just take a minute and begin to thank God for the privilege of having the ability to move and ravish His heart.

There is nothing that will move the Bridegroom's heart more than a heart of love. It is what He desires most. To do His will and follow Him at all costs is what He cherishes most. It is what He died for. He will not relent in His pursuit until He has all of our heart. I mean everything. When we express our love for God by our willingness to go our own way to the mountain of myrrh, then not only will He be deeply moved by it, but He will also praise us for it, just like He does for the Shulamite. This testimony that He gives about her comes directly from her heart of submission to His will. You will notice *two distinct things* that Jesus praises her for:

> *How delightful is your love, my sister, my bride! How much more pleasing is your love than wine, and the fragrance of your perfume than any spice!*
> Song of Solomon 4:10, NIV

1. Her love. The affections of her heart that cause Him to boast in her.
2. Her fragrance. The sweet aroma of her broken and humble heart causes Him to rejoice over her.

The Shulamite's *love* and *fragrant perfume* ravished the heart of the Bridegroom. He has been imparting these two unique qualities in her up until this point on her journey. Do you remember in 1:2, when she declared that Jesus' love is better than wine? But here in 4:10, Jesus now declares that *her* love is better than wine. It's now reversed. There go these best cheerleaders of each other who are deeply in love. They keep boasting about each other and just can't seem to stop!

It's important for us to understand how much Jesus fervently yearns for our love. It's one thing to read about the Shulamite's love for her Beloved, but it's another thing for us to have a heart of love and fragrance for the One whose name is perfumed poured forth (see Song of Solomon 1:3). Jesus is always looking to see whether we long for Him or not. He wants to see if we are in this relationship more for ourselves or for Him. When we give Him our love we give Him all that He desires. We prove our love for someone when we always want to have them at our side. Jesus' pressing question is always this: who is more loved, Him or our reputation, Him or the work of ministry? That is why He always begins His invitation with the words "for My sake."

> *And everyone who has left houses or brothers or sisters or father or mother for My name's sake, shall receive a hundredfold, and inherit eternal life. But many who are first will be last, and the last first.*
>
> Matthew 19:29–30

I personally believe that the message and revelation of the ravished Bridegroom God is going to fill the earth before the second coming of Christ (see Habakkuk 2:14). His fame, His glory, His passion, His beauty and His love will be put on display by the Father. If we never encounter God's ravished heart for us in a personal way, then we fall short of one of the greatest revelations of His heart towards us. It is this revelation that we desperately need in our generation. Something takes place deep in our hearts when we feel cherished by God. Something moves the innermost parts of our souls when we feel special and unique to the heart of God. Something makes us come alive again when we feel desired by and important to the King of glory. It absolutely changes our entire life. It takes us from the pit of despair to the mountain of glory. It takes us from a life of hopelessness to a life of confidence and hope. We don't have to live at a distance anymore (see Song of Solomon 1:7). We are the ones God likes. He really likes us. He really, really likes us. He really, really, really likes us!

> *My dove, my perfect one, is the only one, The only one of her mother, The favorite of the one who bore her. The daughters saw her And called her blessed, The queens and the concubines, And they praised her.*
>
> Song of Solomon 6:9

> *The Lord appeared of old to me, saying: Yes, I have loved you with an everlasting love; Therefore with lovingkindness I have drawn you.*
>
> Jeremiah 31:3

> *As for the saints who are on the earth, They are the*

The Ravished Bridegroom God

> *excellent ones, is whom is all my delight.*
>
> Psalm 16:3

> *For the Lord takes pleasure in His people; He will beautify the humble with salvation.*
>
> Psalm 149:4

Another way to say that God is ravished is to say that He desires us. He's a God of desire! It is what makes Jesus stand out like the bright stars in the nighttime; it's what makes Him stand out like the dazzling rays of sunlight in the daytime. He is so stunning. He desires weak and broken people like us and wants to be with us forever. We are ones pursued by a Lover. We are desired by God!

The God of Burning Desire

Can it be true? Is it possible for the Almighty God to desire humans? Does the God we worship and serve have deep feelings inside His heart? This is one of the great questions of the ages. The answer is only found in a sincere and intentional pursuit of His heart. There are many believers who don't know that God is filled with desire for them. They don't know that He is filled with affections for them. Do you feel unwanted, or do you feel desired in your heart? I believe we have been living too long without feeling God's burning desire in our lives. We have been too content. Simply said, we're too familiar with a God we hardly know. It is so easy to just forget why Jesus, the Lamb, was slain. We forget what motivated Him to suffer at Calvary. We forget what makes Him worthy before the Father and all the hosts of angels. He is worthy because He was wounded for love. He alone walked the hill of Golgotha. He voluntary laid down everything for the sake of love for human beings. It was His holy desire to redeem weak and sinful people back to His Father.

> *And they sang a new song, saying: You are worthy to take the scroll, and to open its seals; For You were*

slain, And have redeemed us to God by Your blood Out of every tribe and tongue and people and nation.
Revelation 5:9

To be redeemed means we are desired and sought after by someone. That someone is Jesus Himself. It means we belong to that person and that He is committed to bring us to a place of completion; a Bride adorned for her Husband. In Song of Solomon 7, we have an incredible passage about the God of burning desire. It reveals His fiery love. It's a love that is not passive. Let us read this passage and get it deep into our spirit by praying and meditating on it. Remember, the Song of Solomon won't help you very much unless you get it into your prayer life. When you read this passage, put your own name there and ask the Holy Spirit to allow you to feel what is being spoken in the text. It's called being inspired by revelation.

I am my beloved's, And his desire is toward me.
Song of Solomon 7:10

What a stunning reality! We are desired as God's Beloved. This passage clearly describes the passionate desire of Jesus' heart. His desire is toward us and not against us. We are no longer rejected, but desired by the most important person on the face of the earth (see Isaiah 54:7–10). Because we belong to our Lover, we are being swept into His desire. The desire of the fiery Bridegroom is like a mighty river that roars with glory. His desire is like a raging fire that utterly consumes. His desire is like peals of thunder that explodes everywhere. His desire is like a crashing wave that pounds all its obstacles. His desire is stronger than any temptation and will remove the deep pain in your heart. He will not give up on you!

What would our Christian life be like without serving a God who has deep feelings and affections? Imagine coming before Him and expressing your love and devotion to Him

The Ravished Bridegroom God

and never feel His affections back. It would be absolutely miserable. It would be like the earth having no color in it. It would be like singing music without feeling the rhythm of it. It would be like pouring out your love to your husband or wife and never receiving love back. It would be one sided. However, feeling desired by God is powerful! It's like an eagle ascending and soaring into the heights. It is like sweet music to the soul. It is like heaven on earth and is a wonderful way to live. Do you believe that God is for you and not against you? Do you believe that His passion for you is much stronger that your passion for Him?

When God created us in His image, were we a big burden to Him? Was He just tolerating us? When Jesus died for us at Calvary, was He forced by His Father? The simple answer is no. We were not a burden to God at any time in our lives. It was His greatest desire and joy to bring us into fellowship with Him. If God could desire and accept us in our absolute darkness before we were saved, why wouldn't He desire and accept us now that we belong to Him? He desires us in the lowest pit and He desires us in the highest glory of our lives. Hallelujah!

We are the object of God's burning desire. He is not distant from us, but is very interested in the daily affairs of our lives. When we experience the burning desire of God's heart, it makes us a people of another age. It enables us to live wholeheartedly for Him and changes our perspective about life. We realize that there is something bigger than our present struggle. Many believers define their lives by their struggle with their sin and failure and not by the burning desire of the One who loves them. We are not the sum total of our most recent struggle, but are loved by God and are lovers of God. It is who we are and it's what we do. There is no mystery as how to grow as a lover of God. We simply need to become students of God's burning desire. We must search out and become an expert of this subject in our hearts. We must discover why God set His burning, passionate affections upon us.

It was Moses, the prophet of God, who had this revelation in his life. He tells us why God set His affections and desire upon us, as he is addressing the children of Israel. Yes, this was a prophetic promise spoken over them, but it's also a prophetic promise for us today in our present generation.

> *For you are a people holy to the Lord your God. The Lord your God has chosen you out of all the peoples on the face of the earth to be his people, his treasured possession. The Lord did not set his affection on you and choose you because you were more numerous than other peoples, for you were the fewest of all peoples. But it was because the Lord loved you and kept the oath he swore to your forefathers that he brought you out with a mighty hand and redeemed you from the land of slavery, from the power of Pharaoh king of Egypt. Know therefore that the Lord your God; he is the faithful God, keeping his covenant of love to a thousand generations of those who love him and keep his commands.*
> Deuteronomy 7:6–9, NIV

God set His affections upon us not because of how great or unique we are. We actually deserved it the least. But He set His love upon us because of His burning affections. He desired us because He is the God of desire. God's burning desire toward us outshines all other loves. What is so stunning about God's desire toward us is how He takes His former enemies and transforms them into voluntary lovers, without violating their free will. He never forces or threatens anyone to obey Him. He simply woos them with His loving affections to win them over. Hosea, the prophet, gives us a picture of this in the way he goes after his unfaithful wife, Gomer. We see this in the book of Hosea.

Pursued By a Lover

Gomer spent her entire life in harlotry. She never knew what true love was. She only knew that she had no value or significance in life and was used and abused at the hands of men. She could not have been at a lower place in her life. But God, the One who burns with desire for humans was not at all intimidated or embarrassed to walk into her dark pit, and get Himself dirty with her. He is a God of the mud, if you know what I mean.

Just when probably everyone else had given up on Gomer, we see the God of burning desire, the One who has the capacity to be ravished steps on to the scene. That is what a true friend is. Just when everyone walks out, a true friend walks in. So what was God's plan for Gomer? What was in His heart? In Hosea 1, God told Hosea to go and marry this filthy harlot so he could feel His unending love for the nation of Israel. Hosea is a picture of Jesus, the Bridegroom God. The Lord was brokenhearted over His beloved Bride, Israel, whom He has loved, cherished and jealously protected only to be scorned and rejected by her. He invites His friend Hosea to share with Him in His suffering by asking him to take "A wife of harlotry" (see Hosea 1:2). So Hosea marries Gomer and enters into the emotions of lovesickness, fury and grief that consume the Bridegroom's heart. Hosea obeys out of love. He is willing to go his way to the mountain of myrrh. He leaves his comfort zone and marries her without questioning his God.

The question that always amazes me is how could a holy God ask a holy prophet to marry a filthy prostitute? Therein lies the hidden mystery of the gospel (see Colossians 2:2–3). God not only had a plan to go and get Gomer for Himself, but He had a divine strategy to win her over. Hosea already took her to be his wife, but she goes right back into prostitution and chases after other lovers. So what is God's strategy to get her back and transform her into a beautiful Bride? The answer is found in Hosea 2. This is one of my favorite chapters in the Word of God. We see *two distinct things* that Jesus, the Bridegroom God, does to win Gomer over:

> ***Therefore, behold, I will hedge up your way with thorns****, And wall her in, So that she cannot find her paths. She will chase her lovers, But not overtake them; Yes, she will seek them, but not find them....*
> Hosea 2:6–7, emphasis added

> *Therefore, behold,* ***I will allure her****, Will bring her into the wilderness, And speak comfort to her.*
> Hosea 2:14, emphasis added

> *And it shall be, in that day, Says the Lord,* ***That you will call Me 'My husband****,' And no longer call Me 'My Master.'*
> Hosea 2:16, emphasis added

The first thing Jesus does is He hedges her in. That means He is making it so that no matter where she goes or what she does, she always feels empty and unsatisfied in her heart. She would chase after other lovers, but would never find fulfillment with them. No matter how hard she tries to be happy and satisfied in her soul, she always comes up short. Basically said, she is miserable. God is reserving the pleasure she was seeking after for Himself. He is jealous over her and will not let anyone else have her. He is a ravished Bridegroom God!

The second thing He does is allure her into the wilderness where she is more vulnerable and reveals Himself to her as a Husband and not a hard taskmaster. The wilderness here in this context refers to a place of divine encounter. It is what she needs. She definitely has a wrong image of God, because of all the ungodly men in her life who abused her womanhood. She never knew what true intimacy is. She has never experienced what a covenant of love is like. So that is why Jesus tells her that she will see Him as her Husband

The Ravished Bridegroom God

and not her Master. It will be a radical shift in her mindset.

This is the God of burning desire at His best. Just as He was deeply moved over the Shulamite in Song of Solomon 4:9, so He's moved over Gomer. He did what no one else can do: He took a filthy prostitute and transformed her into a lovely Bride. It's what sets Him apart as a ravished Bridegroom. He pursued one who was rejected by her family and friends and brought her into a lifelong betrothal. Just as God did this for Gomer, so He has done it for us as well. We have been pursued by a Lover! The God of burning desire has given us significance and destiny. We are the ones He wants! We have been betrothed as His Bride and that's what redefines everything about us. He sees the cry and longing inside us. He has committed Himself to marry us for not just a few years, but for eternity. He is more than glad to have us as His eternal companions.

Let us get back to the journey of the Shulamite in Song of Solomon 4. Remember, she said yes to go to the mountains with her Beloved. She was willing to go her own way to the mountain of myrrh, and it's what caused Jesus, the Bridegroom, to say over her:

You have ravished my heart, My sister, my spouse;
You have ravished my heart with one look of your eyes,
With one link of your necklace.
Song of Solomon 4:9

Do you notice that Jesus was ravished with only one look of her eyes? The words "one look" may be an allusion to the custom of eastern women who, when they walked abroad or spoke to anyone, showed but one eye. The heart of God was moved with her look of devotion towards Him. It wasn't two or three looks of her eyes that ravished His heart, but it was only one look. He is showing the Shulamite how easy He is to please and satisfy. He is telling her that just one simple yes, one simple cry and one act of willingness are enough for Him.

If one glance catches the eyes of the Bridegroom God, then what will a fixed gaze due to Him? Don't you just love this revelation of Jesus' heart? Just as the Shulamite receives the revelation of the ravished Bridegroom in Song of Solomon 4, so will the end–time Church. It will be a clear, precise message that the Holy Spirit will highlight and unfold. He will raise up forerunners and messengers who live and preach the message of the Bridegroom God. They will be called friends of the Bridegroom.

The North and South Winds

As we come to the end of Song of Solomon 4, we discover a unique two–fold prayer of the Shulamite. Her prayer is going to usher her into the greatest test of her life in Song of Solomon 5. Let's take a look at the radical prayer she prays. It will help set the stage for the sudden surprise for what is going to take place in her journey.

> *Awake, O north wind, And come, O south! Blow upon my garden, That its spices may flow out. Let my beloved come to his garden And eat its pleasant fruits.*
> Song of Solomon 4:16

She prayed for the north winds and the south winds to blow upon her garden. The north winds speak of the bitter cold winds of adversity and difficulty. They are the winds that produce the greatest pressure and resistance. They are the storms that teach us to walk by faith and not by feeling and produce the sweet fragrance of Christ in our lives. The Shulamite is willing to fully embrace the Cross as she cries out for the north winds to blow upon her garden, so she will ultimately become Jesus' garden. This prayer will be answered in 5:3–7 as she will go through her ultimate two–fold test. This will be the place of training for her to become a mature Bride, sealed with the fire of the Bridegroom's love (8:6–7).

The Ravished Bridegroom God

The south winds speak of the refreshing winds of blessings that bring comfort and strength. They produce warmness in the air. These are the winds that encourage and refresh the soul while in the midst of the battle. They are the winds that put wings on the weary. The Shulamite is not being selfish at all to ask for the south winds. She is being wise.

These two winds from heaven both play specific roles in her becoming a fragrant garden for her Beloved's pleasure. They are producing wholeheartedness in her. God knows the exact amount of pressure she needs (north and south winds) to help complete her garden. She is becoming very beautiful and unique in the garden of her heart.

When the Shulamite prays for both the north and south winds, it is a very brave prayer. By praying for the north winds, she is inviting adversity into her life. She is basically saying: "God, I am Yours and I give You full permission to do whatever brings pleasure to You in my life. Because I love You, I gladly invite You to come and bring a shaking in my life. Come and change my heart." This is what is meant by her prayer for the north winds. She was extremely bold with this specific prayer.

Have you ever prayed dangerous prayers? Do you ever think about what you are praying for? I can assure you of this: God does not take your prayers lightly. He takes them seriously!

Now the Shulamite is about to enter into a whole new level of romance and dedication through the glory of the north winds that she prayed for. She is willing to have God do whatever He wants in her life. So let us see how Jesus, the Lover of her soul, answers her prayer and what He has planned for her to bring her into divine maturity.

CHAPTER EIGHT

The Fellowship of Sufferings

I have come to my garden, my sister, my spouse; I have gathered my myrrh with my spice; I have eaten my honeycomb with my honey; I have drunk my wine with my milk. I sleep, but my heart is awake; It is the voice of my beloved! He knocks, saying, Open for me, my sister, my love, My dove, my perfect one; For my head is covered with dew, My locks with the drops of the night. I have taken off my robe; How can I put it on again? I have washed my feet; How can I defile them? My beloved put his hand By the latch of the door, And my heart yearned for him. I arose to open for my beloved, And my hands dripped with myrrh, My fingers with liquid myrrh, On the handles of the lock. I opened for my beloved, But my beloved had turned away and was gone. My heart leaped up when he spoke. I sought him, but I could not find him; I called him, but he gave me no answer. The watchmen who went about the city found me. They struck me, they wounded me; The keepers of the walls Took my veil away from me. I charge you, O daughters of Jerusalem, If you find my beloved, That you tell him I am lovesick!

Song of Solomon 5:1–8

How does Jesus respond to the Bride's bold prayer for the north winds to blow upon her garden? He brings her into a two–fold test in Song of Solomon 5:2–7. It will be the ultimate test in her journey. Jesus invites her into a new level of abandonment and dedication, as she enters the fellowship of His sufferings. Remember, because she was willing to follow her Beloved no matter what the cost, she's now emerging from being a Shulamite into being a Bride. She will be referred to as a Bride the rest of the Song of Solomon.

Before we delve into her two–fold test, I want to look at the Bride becoming Jesus' garden.

> *I have come to my garden, my sister, my spouse; I have gathered my myrrh with my spice; I have eaten my honeycomb with my honey; I have drunk my wine with my milk.*
>
> Song of Solomon 5:1

Jesus' Garden

Remember that in chapters 1–4, I referred to her as the Shulamite; but in chapters 5–8, I refer to her as the Bride. She is growing into full maturity and is beginning to do the will of her Beloved rather than her own will. She is focused on His ultimate pleasure and is slowly surrendering her control, as she abides under Jesus' Lordship.

This is a strategic season and great turning point in the Bride's life in the song. The garden of her heart becomes Jesus' garden. It is Jesus Himself who said I have come to my garden. He now sees her as His garden instead of her own garden. She is now living under His ownership. Nine times Jesus uses the word "My" in (5:1). He wants to take over her life completely. This is what He has been after the whole time. Everything she has gone through has been about becoming Jesus' private garden. In Song of Solomon 4:12, Jesus declared that she was a garden. But in Song of Solomon 5:1, He declares that she is His garden. She went from being *a* garden to being *His* garden. That is a powerful testimony from the lips of Jesus about the Bride. This is where you are heading in your prophetic journey. You are learning to fully

The Fellowship of Sufferings

surrender the control of your life to your Beloved. It's the very cry of your heart!

I personally believe that most of our lives are spent being a garden to Jesus and not His garden. We belong to Him and do love Him, but were not fully surrendered to His will and ownership. Being a garden means we are giving Jesus *some access* into the interior life of our hearts and souls. But being Jesus' garden requires humility, submission, obedience and surrender. It means Jesus has *full access* into the interior life of our hearts and souls. He is the One calling the shots and not us.

Let us now see what happens to the Bride as she encounters the most difficult test in her entire life. After Jesus declares that she is now His garden in 5:1, she is found upon her bed sleeping, but her heart is alive and awake.

> ***I sleep, but my heart is awake****; It is the voice of my beloved! He knocks, saying, Open for me, my sister, my love, My dove, my perfect one; For my head is covered with dew, My locks with the drops of the night.*
>
> Song of Solomon 5:2, emphasis added

The Bride is on her bed again. Do you remember back in Song of Solomon 3, when she was on her bed, seeking her Beloved in a time of chastisement? And here in chapter 5, she is seeking her Beloved on her bed again, but this time she is not being disciplined. She is in a good season of mature obedience. Her bed is a distinct place of refuge for her. Do you notice that her heart is awake and not dead? Her heart is alive! This is how she felt on the inside. I believe she is still soaking in the revelation of the ravished Bridegroom. As she is upon her bed, she hears the voice of her Beloved. He is calling her forth into a unique season. Let's read the verse again and see Jesus, the Beloved, speaking to the Bride.

The Divine Invitation

> *I sleep, but my heart is awake; it is the voice of my beloved! He knocks, saying, "Open for me, my sister, my love, my dove, my perfect one; for my head is covered with dew, my locks with the drops of the night."*
> Song of Solomon 5:2

The Bride is being ushered into a two-fold test as an invitation to enter the fellowship of God's sufferings. The first test she faces is the test of Jesus withdrawing His manifest presence from her. He turned away and was gone (5:6). This is how Jesus responded to her loving obedience to open the door for Him. Doesn't sound like a good deal does it? It's not fair. Why did He leave? Was He trying to play hard to get? I don't think so. I believe He has been waiting a long time for this occasion. He has been affirming her and preparing her for this strategic test.

Jesus is seen knocking on the door and inviting the Bride to open up for Him. It is a divine invitation into the fiery furnace of devotion with Him. He is a jealous God who longs for bridal partnership. He is outside her house, knocking upon her door. He is a perfect gentleman; He never forces Himself on her, but takes the initiative and invites her to a deeper life of loyalty and sacrificial love.

Jesus then empowers the Bride to open to Him by calling her by four distinct titles that describe different facets of her intimate relationship with Him. It helps give her confidence to arise and obey. Let us look at these four names:

My Sister–This signifies His identification with her humanity. He endured indescribable sufferings to be like His brethren in all things (see Hebrews 2:17).

My Love–This reminds her of His fervent, tender love for her. He didn't say to her, "you are My disappointing one," but He says, "you are My love."

The Fellowship of Sufferings

My Dove–This speaks of her singleness of mind and loyalty. It speaks of her unique focus. A dove never mates again when their partner dies. He is acknowledging that she is in this relationship until the end.

My Perfect One–This tells us that her cry and sincere intentions are to perfectly obey God. Perfection in this context refers to being mature. I would call it emotional maturity. He declares that she has mature obedience. He sees her cry in secret to love him and defines her life as perfect. Can you see yourself here in the story? Do you realize that Jesus looks at you right now and calls you His perfect one? Will you simply embrace it in your heart?

This is how Jesus is preparing the Bride's heart for her ultimate test. He comes to her as the Man of Sorrows (see Isaiah 53:3), and invites her into the fellowship of His sufferings. When He knocks on the door, He has been out in the long cold night alone. His hair is covered with dew and the drops of the night.

> *I sleep, but my heart is awake; it is the voice of my beloved! He knocks, saying, "Open for me, my sister, my love, my dove, my perfect one; for my head is covered with dew, my locks with the drops of the night."*
> Song of Solomon 5:2

This is a picture of Jesus in Gethsemane. Just as He embraced the Cross in the long lonely night in Gethsemane, He invites her to experience what He experienced. He wants her to identify with His heart. He is calling her to open her heart for Him in order to experience a new measure of abandonment and dedication to Him. He doesn't want her preaching on the power of the cross, but He wants her living in the power of the cross. He longs to be the only goal of her life and not just a means to an end. He not only wants her to be His private garden, but He wants to be the seal of love and fire upon her heart. This is where He is leading her.

As Jesus is knocking and inviting the Bride to open the door of her heart for Him, how does she respond to His invitation?

> *I have taken off my robe; how can I put it on again? I have washed my feet; how can I defile them?*
> Song of Solomon 5:3

Many commentators think the Bride is being disobedient here since she doesn't immediately respond and get out of her bed and open the door for her Beloved. But I believe she is actually being obedient in her heart. When she says that she had taken off her robe and didn't want to put it on again, she is already confident that she is the righteousness of Christ Jesus (see Isaiah 61:10). She already took off her defiled garments and put on His garments of righteousness. She refuses to wear her old garments and live in compromise. She is not going back to her old path. It is not a statement of compromise but resolve. She not only refuses to put on her robe again, but she refuses to put on her shoes as well. She is not lazy, but does not want to defile her feet through compromise. If she were compromising, then this passage would have a totally different meaning.

As Jesus is outside the front door and she is inside her house upon her bed, He then puts His hand on the latch of the door. He is taking this invitation to a deeper level.

Jesus is not just knocking, but He is now prying open the latch door. In fact, He thrusts His hand through the latch opening. He is jealous for her. He can't restrain the very flame of love and zeal from His Bride. So how does she respond? What is happening inside her soul? Let us take a glimpse and see.

> *My beloved put his hand by the latch of the door, and my heart yearned for him. I arose to open for my beloved, and my hands dripped with myrrh, my fingers with liquid myrrh, on the handles of the lock.*
> Song of Solomon 5:4–5

The Bride's Yearning Heart

If the Bride is being disobedient to the invitation of her Beloved, than why is her heart pictured as yearning for Him, as she arises to open the door? She has a yearning heart. There is a life of glory going on inside her soul. Maybe others can't see the secret cry of her heart, but God can. Remember, it's her cry and obedient heart which is her greatest weapon she possess, and only Jesus Himself can see that cry!

The Bride arises to open the door for Him. She just can't take it anymore. As she walks over to the front door, she puts her hand on the latch and feels the oil of myrrh dripping on it. Remember, Jesus had just put His hand on the latch of the door. It's overflowing with myrrh. Jesus is the myrrh of heaven. His name is perfume poured forth (1:3). The Beloved leaves a distinct mark for her with liquid myrrh. Remember, myrrh is a burial spice, and it speaks of death to self and a commitment to embrace the Cross. That is exactly what she is doing here as she fulfills her commitment to go up to the mountains (4:6).

Jesus putting His hand through the latch refers to Him helping the Bride unlock the door of her heart. It is the nail–scarred hands of the Lamb of God. Here, we not only see the power of the Lord's death, but we see the smell and fragrance of His death in the myrrh that He left upon the handle. The hand that gripped the latch is the same hand that embraces her under the apple tree (2:6).

She not only verbally says yes to the mountains, but she is literally doing it. She fulfills the call of Song of Solomon 2. She had the big cry in her heart and said yes in Song of Solomon 4:6, and now she follows through in her commitment. She arises in full obedience to open the door for her Beloved.

I just love the language of the Bride's heart as she is pictured rising from her bed. Remember, in Song of Solomon 3, she was upon her bed reflecting from her mistake? Now she is on her bed again, but this time she's not reflecting but yearning. She declares that her heart yearns for Him. The Vulgate translation says "My soul melted when He spoke." Her heart is being tenderized by the gentle voice of the Beloved. She is not passive to His request to open the door of her heart, but yearns and longs to arise to Jesus of Gethsemane.

Are you starting to realize that this is your journey in the Song of Solomon? Do you see yourself here in the story? You are a lover of God. You long to do whatever it takes to find your Beloved. You will say yes to the fellowship of His sufferings. You will embrace the cross in your life. Your heart is beginning to yearn and pound for the One who bears the marks of slaughter (see Revelation 5:6). You will arise in full obedience to the voice that's beckoning from heaven, no matter what the cost. Amen!

The Bride's First Test: The Withdrawal of God's Presence

> *I opened for my beloved, But my beloved had turned away and was gone. My heart leaped up when he spoke. I sought him, but I could not find him; I called him, but he gave me no answer.*
>
> Song of Solomon 5:6

This is the specific path Jesus, the Beloved, has wisely chosen for her. It's the mountain of myrrh that she's now climbing. This is how He is producing a deeper resolution in her soul. He is developing a confidence in her that will make her strong and bold on the inside. He knows that she can take it, but He wants her to discover that, to see how much is really deposited within her. When she realizes that He has turned away after she opened the front door, what is the response inside her heart? Is she shocked? Is she confused? Is she offended?

The Fellowship of Sufferings

No, she isn't offended. What a testimony. She is pictured seeking after her Beloved, and calling upon Him in prayer. She says, "I sought him, but I could not find him; I called him but he gave me no answer." Doesn't that sound familiar? Do you remember back in Song of Solomon 3 when the same thing happened? She was seeking after her Beloved, but she couldn't find Him. But this crisis in Song of Solomon 5 is much different from the other time. Last time, Jesus withdrew His manifest presence because of her fear and refusal to go to the mountains with Him. That made sense. But now He withdraws His manifest presence because of her loving obedience. That doesn't make sense. Have you ever come to a place in your walk with your Beloved where He just doesn't make sense? You wonder what He is up to. You wonder if you have done something wrong to cause Him to turn away and disappear. This happens to every Shulamite who loves God and wants to become a mature Bride!

The Silence of God: Our Escort into God's Heart

Just as the Lord hid Himself from the Bride on her journey, so He does the same with us. He hides Himself from the obedient heart, not because of some sin or an attack of the devil, but because He wants to draw out the yearning of our hearts in a deeper and more definitive way. This may not make sense, especially when we are actually in the midst of it. It can produce many questions against the One we love. Nobody likes pain and adversity. Nobody likes when the heavens are silent. But it is a divine escort into God's heart if we yield and cooperate with Him in the process. God is not passive in our circumstances. So we must constantly be looking for the power of God to break through. Silence causes us to cry out. It produces a groan!

When God is silent and He withdraws His glorious presence, we soon discover what is on the inside of us. Just when we thought we were growing into full maturity and becoming strong in our spirit, we then discover the hidden accusations rising to the surface. The spirit of offense begins to find its way into the situation. We feel like we are not being treated fairly even though we are doing His will. But let's understand that God is being totally fair in all His decisions regarding us. He is very kind, very wise and has thought through everything we will ever go through. He has a divine purpose in it. He is Sovereign and can do as He pleases. We can count on this prophetic promise: He is absolutely faithful in all that He does.

> *I will proclaim the name of the Lord. Oh, praise the greatness of our God! He is the rock, his works are perfect, and all his ways are just. A faithful God who does no wrong, upright and just is he.*
> Deuteronomy 32:3–4, NIV

Is it possible that God's silence can serve as an escort into His love? I believe it can. There is a place of discovery and adventure during the seasons of God's silence. It's a wonderful, but painful place to be. I believe for many of us, we think silence from heaven means:

- God must be angry at me.
- God is disappointed with me and doesn't talk to me anymore.
- God is rejecting me because I did something wrong.
- God is making my life difficult.
- God doesn't really care about me.
- God has forgotten all about me.

These accusations that lie deep inside our soul are what Jesus is personally after; He longs to root them out of us. He is jealous that we have no accusations or offense against Him during the dark night of our souls. It is the silence of a hiding God that must do its work in our soul. He is training our hearts in the silent wilderness. Not only is He going to expose the offense inside us during the times of silence, but He is going to ask us a few simple, yet provoking questions in this strategic season. These questions are like a bright light that penetrates through all the different pockets in our hearts. They are questions that reveal our true motives on our spiritual journey, helping us discover what it is we are really after. Simply put, they are questions from the One who is love.

1. Will you still love Me and follow me even if you don't feel My love or presence?
2. Are you really in this relationship for Me or for yourself?
3. Will you be mine even if I withhold the things you desire most?
4. Will you still love and trust Me when you are disappointed by your circumstances?
5. Will you obey My will no matter how difficult the challenge?

These are painful questions that we all must wrestle with. I don't know about you, but after going over these five questions, I just say, "ouch!" I have wrestled with some of these questions during a great time of testing when the heavens were silent, and I have failed miserably most of the time. Now that doesn't mean I don't love God, but I have discovered that a lot of my seeking has been after other things (lesser pleasures) and not love itself (ultimate pleasure).

Three Examples From Scripture

I want to look at three men in the Old Testament who went through tremendous pain in their souls. They faced the silence of heaven, even when they sought after God, just like the Shulamite. They faced confusion. They felt abandoned and disappointed by God as they were in the season of the wilderness. The first person we will look at is Job. Listen to his bitter cry and complaint.

Then Job replied: "How long will you torment me and crush me with words? Ten times now you have reproached me; shamelessly you attack me. If it is true that I have gone astray, my error remains my concern alone. If indeed you would exalt yourselves above me and use my humiliation against me, then know that God has wronged me and drawn his net around me." Though I cry, 'I've been wronged!' I get no response; though I call for help, there is no justice. He has blocked my way so I cannot pass; he has shrouded my paths in darkness. He has stripped me of my honor and removed the crown from my head. He tears me down on every side till I am gone; he uproots my hope like a tree. His anger burns against me; he counts me among his enemies...I know that my Redeemer lives, and that in the end he will stand upon the earth. And after my skin has been destroyed, yet in my flesh I will see God; I myself will see him with my own eyes—I, and not another. How my heart yearns within me!

Job 19:1–11, 25–27, NIV

This is just a glimpse of what Job suffered as a righteous man, not including losing his ten children, all of his flocks and herds, all of his servants, and he broke out with sores and boils on his body. Let's listen to his pain and complaint inside his heart regarding heaven being silent. He says, "though I cry, 'I've been wronged!' I get no response; though I call for help, there is no justice" (see Job 19:7). That was his ultimate pain: heaven was silent. God was not responding at all to his cry for help. Was He not interested? Was He not being compassionate? Was He unfair to Job during his most vulnerable time? Job will have to discover for himself. He is being trained in the wilderness to love, trust and grow into maturity with God. In Job 19, we have a simple overview of what Job faced inside his heart as he sought God in his obedience:

- He felt tormented by God (19:2, 21).
- He was stripped of his honor (19:9).

The Fellowship of Sufferings

- He was counted as an enemy to God (19:11).
- His close friends forgot about him (19:13–14).
- His maidservants counted him a stranger (19:15).
- His servant despised him (19:16).
- His wife and children were offended at him (19:17).
- Little boys in the streets ridiculed him (19:18).
- He was nothing but skin and bones (19:20).

What was the point of all Job's suffering and feeling abandoned by God? I believe it comes down to the fact that he was changed. God never gave Job the answers he asked for. Instead, Job got more of God. Job was changed! In Job 42, we find his own confession about what he learned during his time of suffering, when heaven was silent. He mentions *four things* that changed his life.

1. He declares that God can do everything. He already knew this in his mind, but now it was very real in his heart. He declares that no purpose of His can be stopped.

I know that You can do everything, and that no purpose of Yours can be withheld from You.
Job 42:2

2. He declares that he uttered with his mouth that which he didn't understand. But now he has clear understanding about the ways of God.

You asked, 'Who is this who hides counsel without knowledge?' Therefore I have uttered what I did not understand, things too wonderful for me, which I did not know.
Job 42:3

3. He declares that he heard about God with his ears, but now he sees who He is. He experienced beholding

God in a new and fresh way.

I have heard of You by the hearing of the ear, but now my eye sees You.
Job 42:5

4. He repents in dust and ashes. He regrets accusing the leadership of God over his life. And in Job 40, he tells God that he will now put his hand over his mouth and proceed no further. He will keep silent and not accuse Him anymore.

Therefore I abhor myself, and repent in dust and ashes.
Job 42:6

Then Job answered the Lord and said: "Behold, I am vile; what shall I answer You? I lay my hand over my mouth. Once I have spoken, but I will not answer; yes, twice, but I will proceed no further.
Job 40:3–6

Job cried out to God night after night during the dark night of his soul, yet he got no response at all. Then suddenly, in Job 38, we see the Lord step on to the scene as He asks Job thirty-five questions about His surpassing greatness in creation; then Job is completely silenced. It's immediately after these penetrating questions that Job's perspective is changed. His life was restored completely. In fact, the Lord blessed the latter days of Job more than his beginning (see Job 42:12). Job died an old man, full of days (see Job 42:17). Job was changed!

The second person we will look at is David. Listen to his bitter cry and complaint.

How long, O Lord? Will you forget me forever? How long will you hide your face from me? How long must I wrestle with my thoughts and every day have sorrow in

The Fellowship of Sufferings

my heart? How long will my enemy triumph over me? Look on me and answer, O Lord my God. Give light to my eyes, or I will sleep in death; my enemy will say, "I have overcome him," and my foes will rejoice when I fall. But I trust in your unfailing love; my heart rejoices in your salvation. I will sing to the Lord, for he has been good to me.

Psalm 13:1–6, NIV

Do you notice the key question that consumed David during his painful season of silence in the wilderness? He said the famous words–"how long?" He asked that question four times. He probably thought that his sorrows would never end. He felt abandoned and forgotten by God. He felt God had withdrawn His presence from him for no good reason. He was in torment in his thought life about this. That is where the wrestling was taking place. He felt defeated at the hands of his enemies. What was the point of David's pain and suffering? Why did God withdraw His presence and not respond to his cry? It's because he was learning *two distinct things* about the heart of God:

1. He learned to trust in the unfailing love of the Lord, even when things didn't make sense.

But I trust in your unfailing love; my heart rejoices in your salvation.

Psalm 13:5, NIV

2. He came to understand the goodness of God in his life. It would become the song of his life in his journey. David was changed!

I will sing to the Lord, for he has been good to me.

Psalm 13:6, NIV

The third person we will look at is Jeremiah. Listen to his bitter cry and complaint.

I am the man who has seen affliction by the rod of His wrath. He has led me and made me walk in darkness and not in light. Surely He has turned His hand against me time and time again throughout the day. He has aged my flesh and my skin, and broken my bones. He has besieged me and surrounded me with bitterness and woe. He has set me in dark places like the dead of long ago. He has hedged me in so that I cannot get out; he has made my chain heavy. Even when I cry and shout, he shuts out my prayer. He has blocked my ways with hewn stone; he has made my paths crooked. He has been to me a bear lying in wait, like a lion in ambush. He has turned aside my ways and torn me in pieces; he has made me desolate. He has bent His bow and set me up as a target for the arrow. He has caused the arrows of His quiver to pierce my loins. I have become the ridicule of all my people–their taunting song all the day. He has filled me with bitterness, he has made me drink wormwood. He has also broken my teeth with gravel, and covered me with ashes. You have moved my soul far from peace; I have forgotten prosperity. And I said, "My strength and my hope have perished from the Lord." Remember my affliction and roaming, the wormwood and the gall. My soul still remembers and sinks within me. This I recall to my mind, therefore I have hope. Through the Lord's mercies we are not consumed, because His compassions fail not. They are new every morning; great is Your faithfulness. "The Lord is my portion," says my soul, "Therefore I hope in Him!" The Lord is good to those who wait for Him, to the soul who seeks Him.

Lamentations 3:1–25

Jeremiah singles himself out as the man who has seen affliction. I believe he really meant it. I can totally relate to him. Jeremiah's ultimate pain is similar to Job's, David's and the Bride's. He says, "Even when I call out or cry for help, He shuts out my prayer" (see Lamentations 3:8). That was his pain–heaven was silent. No matter how much he

The Fellowship of Sufferings

prayed it seemed to have no effect. Even though he cried for help, his prayer was not heard. Here is a simple overview of what he had to face in his season in the wilderness when he was seeking God with all of his heart:

- He was the man who had seen affliction (3:1).
- God turned His hand against him (3:2).
- His skin and bones were deteriorating (3:4).
- He dwelt in darkness (3:6).
- He felt forsaken and abandoned by God (3:8).
- He felt helpless (3:11).
- He was a laughingstock to his friends (3:14).
- He was trampled in dust (3:16).
- He forgot what prosperity was (3:17).
- His strength and hope had perished through his afflictions (3:18–19).

What was the point of Jeremiah's pain and suffering? Why did God shut out His prayer? It's because God wanted to reveal *five distinct things* about His heart to him:

1. He got a fresh revelation of the Lord's mercy. He knew that he would never be consumed. That's what changed his perspective.

Through the Lord's mercies we are not consumed, because His compassions fail not.
Lamentations 3:22

2. He saw the greatness of God's faithfulness through all of his pain and adversity. He probably had a little understanding of God's faithfulness, but now he's receiving the revelation of God's *great* faithfulness.

They are new every morning; Great is Your faithfulness.
Lamentations 3:23

3. He understood that God is extremely good to those who wait and hope for Him, especially when they cry for help and seem to get no answer.

The Lord is good to those whose hope is in him, to the one who seeks him; it is good to wait quietly for the salvation of the Lord.
Lamentations 3:25–26, NIV

4. He knew God would not fail or abandon anyone who loves Him. He understood that no matter how difficult the pain, the Lord would show compassion.

For men are not cast off by the Lord forever. Though he brings grief, he will show compassion, so great is his unfailing love.
Lamentations 3:31–32, NIV

5. He understood that God does not willingly bring affliction or grief to the sons of men. It's not His first choice. Through all of his afflictions, we can see that Jeremiah was changed!

For he does not willingly bring affliction or grief to the children of men.
Lamentations 3:33, NIV

I believe we all can relate to Job, David and Jeremiah, who felt abandoned by God and struggled when heaven was silent. We must understand that suffering is a profound mystery! Many times it seems to not make sense at the time. But let's not get offended at the Lord's perfect leadership. He knows exactly what He is doing. We are not to make things happen in the season of silence. He is doing a deep work to bring change within us. That's the point!

Unanswered prayers are not unheard. The Lord keeps a file for our prayers, and they are not blown away by the wind, but are treasured in the King's archives. Every single cry and prayer is recorded in heaven. One thing we can count on is this: heaven may be silent at times, but the heart of God never stops beating. Hallelujah!

Let us quickly learn what God is trying to teach us in the wilderness. Let us discover an attribute of His heart during our deepest pain and difficulty. Let us realize that even tragedy has an ultimate goal because we are being changed by it. Job learned of God's faithfulness. He had tremendous confidence that His Redeemer lived and that in the end He was going to stand upon the earth (see Job 19:25). David learned of God's unfailing love. He knew he could count and rely upon it (see Psalm 13:5). Jeremiah learned of God's mercy. He knew that he would not be consumed or get what he deserved (see Lamentations 3:22).

The Bride's Second Test: The Pain of Mistreatment

The second test the Bride will face concerns the watchmen who strike her and wound her. This test is about mistreatment. Silence and mistreatment is her two-fold test that she has to go through. They are the obstacles that are trying to hinder and distract her love for her Beloved. Let us continue in Song of Solomon 5 and see what happens to her in this situation, and how she responds during her second test.

> *I sleep, but my heart is awake; it is the voice of my beloved! He knocks, saying, Open for me, my sister, my love, my dove, my perfect one; for my head is covered with dew, my locks with the drops of the night... I opened for my beloved, but my beloved had turned away and was gone. My heart leaped up when he spoke. I sought him, but I could not find him; I called him, but he gave me no answer. The watchmen who went about the city found me. They struck me, they wounded me; The keepers of the walls Took my veil away from me.*
>
> Song of Solomon 5:2, 6–7

After the Bride had opened the door for her Beloved, she realizes that He is gone and disappeared. So she immediately leaves her house and is out in the streets of Jerusalem, searching for her Beloved. We saw her do this back in Song of Solomon 3 and we are seeing her do it again here in Song of Solomon 5. Again, she was yearning and intently looking for her Beloved, when suddenly, the watchmen found her as they made their rounds in the city. As we already looked at the David watchmen in Song of Solomon 3, now we are going to look at the Saul watchmen. Remember, the watchmen are the leaders in the Body of Christ who exercise spiritual authority.

The watchmen find her. As they are on duty, they notice her out in the city of Jerusalem. I don't know if they are intentionally looking for her or if they just happen to see her. But they find her. What do they do when they find her? Last time they helped her as she was in trouble. But this time their reaction is much different. That is why I believe they are the Saul watchmen. I don't believe they are the same leaders as before. Let us look at three distinct things they did to the Bride in Song of Solomon 5:7.

1. They struck her.
2. They wounded her.
3. They take away her veil.

Doesn't sound like good leadership to me. Instead of helping her, they try to destroy her. That reminds me of Saul, who was jealous and threatened by the presence of David as he tried to kill him with a spear (see 1 Samuel 19:10). What was on the inside of him would come out at the right time with the right amount of pressure.

Let's look in more detail at what the watchmen do to the Bride. First, they struck her. The Hebrew word for "struck" is *nakah*. It means to punish, to strike, to smite, to attack and destroy, to give stripes or a wound. They might have physically abused her, but it's not fully clear. Second, they wounded her. The Hebrew word for "wounded" is *patsa*. It means to bruise, to split and to deeply wound. It describes reproaches of the tongue that cause deep hurt and pain. It describes insults, slander and gossip. I do believe there was verbal abuse involved. This is the most hurtful and painful abuse. It deeply wounds the spirit man. Third, they take away her veil. The Hebrew word for "veil" is *radiyd*. It means to spread a veil over the head. It also speaks of a robe or covering. The same Hebrew term veil is rendered "shawl" (NAS), "cloak" (NIV) and "mantle" (KJV).

A veil was a covering for the head usually worn by women. It was a token of modesty (see Genesis 24:65). When the watchmen take away the Bride's veil, they take away her dignity. The removal of the veil was part of a humiliating assault of the King's beloved. They take it off rudely to make her feel shame and embarrassment. This was nothing but dishonor and shame. It was the greatest indignity to an eastern woman. It is very possible that these watchmen heard about her spiritual progress and decided to cause havoc in her life. They turned against her. They are not policeman guarding the peace of the city. If they were, then what are they doing wounding and beating up someone? They are mistreating an innocent farm girl. She did nothing to deserve this. She wasn't looking for trouble, but she was looking for her Beloved, the One she loved, admired and adored.

Have you ever found yourself in this situation, where you are simply doing your very best to seek hard after God, and yet find yourself being mistreated at the hands of spiritual leaders? It's very painful isn't it? Now, I don't have any energy to focus upon the weaknesses and faults of spiritual leaders and put blame upon them for hurting innocent believers. Actually, there is no one who is innocent. Every human being is guilty and has fallen short of the glory of God. But, I do sadly realize that there is a lot of spiritual abuse and mistreatment taking place under leaders in the body of Christ. It's a sad testimony!

Mistreatment is a part of our journey into wholehearted love. Nobody who loves Jesus will escape it. I am not talking about any form of abuse, but am talking about treading the same path that Jesus tread. Just as He was mistreated and misunderstood, so we will be also. Just as He encountered unfairness at the hands of evil men, so we will face the same thing. In fact, Peter tells us that part of our calling in God is to suffer for doing good. It's called unjust suffering. I believe the book of 1 Peter gives us the biblical response to unjust suffering. We are to bear up under the pain of it because we are aware that the Lover of our soul is watching and recording every movement of our hearts. Listen to what Peter has to say to every believer who loves God and wants to follow after Him. It's very challenging!

> *For it is commendable if a man bears up under the pain of unjust suffering because he is conscious of God. But how is it to your credit if you receive a beating for doing wrong and endure it? But if you suffer for doing good and you endure it, this is commendable before God. To this you were called, because Christ suffered for you, leaving you an example, that you should follow in his steps. "He committed no sin, and no deceit was found in his mouth." When they hurled their insults at him, he did not retaliate; when he suffered, he made no threats. Instead, he entrusted himself to him who judges justly. He himself bore our sins in his body on the tree, so that we might die to sins and live for righteousness; by his wounds you have been healed.*
> 1 Peter 2:19–24, NIV

Pain is the great equalizer because everyone experiences it in this life. We don't have to look for trouble, for trouble will find us. Paul the Apostle tells us that through many tribulations we *must* enter His Kingdom (see Acts 14:22). Discouragement is no respecter or persons and seems to attack us from all sides without any notice. Being wounded in the house of friends is part of God's pattern that even Jesus endured (see Psalm 55:12–21). When we are in the very midst of it, we have a great opportunity to love Jesus and not be offended. Anything that prepares us to not be offended when we stand before God on the last day seems wise. We have an opportunity to allow the Lord to make us beautiful in the places of our deepest pain. He desires for us to be fully alive and restored on the inside rather than trying to protect our hearts from experiencing pain. It is an opportunity to fellowship with the crucified One and wait for the Father to come to us in resurrection power.

Mistreatment that comes from the hand of God seems to be so selected, so tailored for the one to whom it is sent. When it happens, we don't understand it and struggle to accept it. Basically, we are fighting the power of the Cross inside us.

There are two primary sources of most of our misery and turmoil in the face of mistreatment: blame and pride. This is what keeps us from wholeness and restoration. Instead of looking to heaven and focusing upon what the Lord wants to do in us, we usually focus upon the people mistreating us and start blaming them and accusing them. Also, the character qualities that we hate in others who mistreat us are the same things at work in us. It's called deep seated pride. But here is the good news: we don't have to live this type of lifestyle. Let us begin to cry out and ask God to help us with blaming and being proud, and choose to humble ourselves before Him (see James 4:10).

Once again, I will look to David, who is a prime example of one who faced mistreatment at the hands of the righteous, yet he chose to not be offended and allowed God to work deeply in his heart. He never lost his focus in the process. He gives us a proper response of how to face mistreatment.

> *Let a righteous man strike me—it is a kindness; let him rebuke me—— it is oil on my head. My head will not refuse it. Yet my prayer is ever against the deeds of*

evildoers.
Psalm 141:5, NIV

David highlights two important words: "strike" and "rebuke." Just like the Bride, he is facing the test of mistreatment. He is being struck and rebuked. And the most difficult part of the test is that it's not coming from the unrighteous, but it's coming from the righteous. What was the key he learned during his test? What did he do right in this situation? He didn't take revenge into his own hands. He received mistreatment as an opportunity to grow on the inside, and he knew that he would inherit a blessing. That was his focus. He did not refuse the harsh mistreatment from the hands of the righteous, but he took it. He welcomed it as an opportunity to demonstrate his love for his Beloved. He knew by revelation that it wasn't evil being done to him, but it was kindness. He also knew that it was for his personal benefit. He said it was like oil on his head. I would say that's a depth of great maturity.

It was Jesus who personally told us that we are to love, do good, bless, and pray for those who mistreat us. He knew it would happen, so in His kindness, He lets us know beforehand and gives us a simple solution.

> *But I say to you who hear: Love your enemies, do good to those who hate you, bless those who curse you, and pray for those who spitefully use you. To him who strikes you on the one cheek, offer the other also. And from him who takes away your cloak, do not withhold your tunic either. Give to everyone who asks of you. And from him who takes away your goods do not ask them back. And just as you want men to do to you, you also do to them likewise.*
> Luke 6:27–31

We can come to a place of victory in the midst of being wounded and mistreated just like David and just as we are

The Fellowship of Sufferings

learning from the response of the Bride in Song of Solomon 5. We have a big God with a big heart, and He is more than willing to help us embrace any difficulty that comes our way and find freedom in the midst of it. He desires to heal and restore us. When we come into contact with pain and helplessness, it's an entry point into wholeness.

Why God Allows Mistreatment

I want to give a simple list of why the Lord allows us to be mistreated in our journey with Him. I encourage you to take these points and develop them even more, so you can be a forerunner and help those who are struggling and are offended at God's loving leadership:

- He is teaching us the depths of His heart. We discover Him in deep places of pain and difficulty.
- He is building and changing us into Christ–likeness. We are being trained to be merciful.
- He is teaching us to look at Him and not the people who are mistreating us, to have heaven's perspective.
- He is exposing the false foundations within the vineyard of our hearts. Mistreatment reveals what's really down deep inside us. We don't really know who we are until we get bumped by someone. It brings out the real you.
- He is teaching us how to embrace humility. When we are mistreated by someone, it reveals how much we fight for the need to be right. So here is the key question we must ask ourselves when facing unfairness and mistreatment: would you rather be right or be right with God?
- He is teaching us emotional and spiritual maturity. We are learning to grow up and become Jesus' lovely Bride, fully surrendered to His Lordship.

- He is intending something good to come out of it, just like He did in the life of Joseph. Joseph was thrown into prison for no good reason. It wasn't fair. Yet, even though man intended evil against him, God intended good. He had a higher purpose. Joseph went from the dungeon to the palace.
- He knows something we don't. Something bigger is going on. We won't fully understand it all until we see the One who burns with desire and passion for us. He is doing something in our spirits for all eternity (see Romans 8:18).

I think we can clearly see that pain and mistreatment can become a great blessing in our lives as we respond rightly. Here is the heart of the matter: we may not have any control over what is happening to us, but we have a great deal of control over our reaction to what is happening to us.

Let us now look at how the Bride responds after she is mistreated by the watchmen. Remember, she is going through a two-fold test. She lost her Beloved and could not find Him after searching for Him in the streets of Jerusalem. And she is mistreated by the Saul watchmen. Does she take this opportunity to grow in love or does she get angry and offended?

> *The watchmen who went about the city found me. They struck me, they wounded me; the keepers of the walls took my veil away from me. I charge you, O daughters of Jerusalem, if you find my beloved, that you tell him I am lovesick!*
>
> Song of Solomon 5:7–8

The Bride is Lovesick

She is lovesick! That's her heart response. She is not offended at her Beloved, nor is she offended at the watchmen. What an amazing place she is at within her own soul. When

The Fellowship of Sufferings

she says that she is lovesick, do you notice who she is talking to? She is talking to the Daughters of Jerusalem. Remember, they are believers, but are not fully committed like the Bride and are living at a distance from the Beloved.

When she tells the Daughters of Jerusalem that if they see her Beloved, to let Him know that she is lovesick, she uses a powerful word. She says, "I charge you." The Hebrew word for "charge" is *shaba*. It means to take an oath, to swear as if by repeating a declaration seven times. This oath shows the strength of her love. It shows her loyalty and firm commitment. She uses the word charge two other times in the song (see Song of Solomon 2:7; 8:4).

The Bride did not lose her focus while under pressure; she's lovesick. This is what silence and mistreatment produced in her life. It is the outworking of the first commandment, which is to love the Lord with all of our heart, soul, mind and strength. This lovesickness was birthed in the fiery furnace of her two-fold test. She not only passed the test, but she came out of it on fire for Her Lover. Her heart grew larger as she revealed that she was in it for love all the way. It was her primary goal. The word lovesick is mentioned two times in the song (2:5; 5:8). The Hebrew word for "lovesick" is *chalah*. It means to be in anguish, to become weak or sick and to travail. It is a picture of someone who is wounded for love. It is a picture of someone who can't bear it any longer and can't hold in how they feel on the inside. It is a picture of a heart that has been conquered by a love from another age. Her heart is captured and is ready to explode. She is lovesick. That's her testimony!

Jesus wanted her to know Him in the place of difficulty, as He did it all for love. He wanted her to experience it for herself.

How did the Daughters of Jerusalem respond to the charge (oath) the Bride made concerning her Beloved? Remember, she told them that if they found her Beloved, to let Him know that she's lovesick (5:8). Let us hear what they have to say:

> *What is your beloved more than another beloved, O fairest among women? What is your beloved more than another beloved, that you so charge us?*
> Song of Solomon 5:9

They want to know why they are being charged to consider the glory and uniqueness of the Bride's Beloved. They ask the same question two times. I believe The Complete Jewish Bible translation says it best.

> *How does the man you love differ from any other, you most beautiful of women? How does the man you love differ from any other that you should give us this charge?*
> Song of Solomon 5:9, The Complete Jewish Bible

They basically want to know what makes Jesus so distinct and unique that they should give up their present lifestyles and follow after Him. They want proof of His supreme beauty. They want to know what God is like. They want to know why she loves Him so much, especially after what she just went through. Maybe their thinking to themselves, "why are you so loyal to Him? What do you understand about Him that we don't?" They cannot understand this kind of radical devotion. They must be shocked. They probably thought she would be offended at her Beloved and would be complaining to them. They probably thought she would want to take revenge on the watchmen. But that's not the case for her; she's now emerging and becoming a mature Bride!

So how does the Bride respond back to the question of the Daughters of Jerusalem, who want to know what God is like? Her answer is found in Song of Solomon 5:10–16. She paints a portrait of the beauty of Jesus in this passage. She is exploding on the inside. She gives such an ardent expression of the glory and beauty and majesty of her Beloved.

The Fellowship of Sufferings

It is one of the most powerful revelations that she receives. She uses metaphors of the human body to convey truths of His beauty and splendor. Her testimony of Jesus' beauty so moves the Daughters of Jerusalem that they no longer ask, "what is your Beloved" (5:9), but they ask, "where is your beloved" (6:1). They no longer questioned who He was, but now they want to follow after Him with the Bride. They could not stand it any longer. Something was being stirred in them in a very dynamic way at the life and testimony of the Bride. She was modeling what a forerunner does in their walk with Jesus. They not only overcome the spirit of offense, but they give testimony of God's beauty while under divine pressure. Let us hear from the lips of the Daughters of Jerusalem. Do notice their change of posture and tone after the Bride unveils Jesus' surpassing beauty. They were changed!

> *Where has your beloved gone, O fairest among women? Where has your beloved turned aside, that we may seek him with you?*
>
> Song of Solomon 6:1

They asked the same question twice again. They liked being repetitive. What a change! They wanted to seek after the Beloved along with the Bride. They wanted to know where He was. They longed to meet and know the One in whom the Bride just described in Song of Solomon 5.

I want to encourage you to study and meditate upon Jesus' beauty in Song of Solomon 5:10–16. Please take some time and go through it and let it ignite a flame within your own soul, just like it did for the Daughters of Jerusalem. You will soon discover that Jesus is radiant, dazzling, and chief among ten thousand (see Song of Solomon 5:10). He is altogether lovely. There is none like Him.

Looking Ahead

In Song of Solomon 6, we have the revelation of the Bride's beauty and her spiritual identity. She is pictured as being beautiful, lovely, and awesome as an army with banners. She is also called being God's favorite one.

> *O my love, you are as beautiful as Tirzah, lovely as Jerusalem, awesome as an army with banners...My dove, my perfect one, is the only one, the only one of her mother, the favorite of the one who bore her. The daughters saw her and called her blessed, the queens and the concubines, and they praised her.*
> Song of Solomon 6:4, 9, emphasis added

In Song of Solomon 7, we have the divine partnership between the Bride and the Bridegroom. The Bride has a cry and longing to give her love away to her Beloved, in the vineyards. They are becoming one in heart. They are pictured as doing everything together in love, the perfect picture of bridal partnership. Do notice the words "let us" mentioned four times in 7:11–12.

> *I am my beloved's, and his desire is toward me. Come, my beloved, let us go forth to the field; let us lodge in the villages. Let us get up early to the vineyards; let us see if the vine has budded, whether the grape blossoms are open, and the pomegranates are in bloom. There I will give you my love. The mandrakes give off a fragrance, and at our gates are pleasant fruits, all manner, new and old, which I have laid up for you, my beloved.*
> Song of Solomon 7:10–13

Now we are going to come to the climax of the final chapter in the Song of Solomon. It will leave your heart awestruck at where the Bride ends up in her spiritual journey with her Beloved.

Questions to Ponder

1. Do you desire to be Jesus' garden? What practical steps are you going to take?
2. Do you fully desire God even if He withholds the things you treasure most?
3. Do you find your heart being offended or lovesick when you're being mistreated? Why?

CHAPTER NINE

The Bridal Seal of Fire

Who is this coming up from the wilderness, leaning upon her beloved? I awakened you under the apple tree. There your mother brought you forth; there she who bore you brought you forth. Set me as a seal upon your heart, as a seal upon your arm; for love is as strong as death, jealousy as cruel as the grave; its flames are flames of fire, a most vehement flame. Many waters cannot quench love, nor can the floods drown it. If a man would give for love all the wealth of his house, it would be utterly despised.

Song of Solomon 8:5–7

She did it! The Bride has come to the final chapter (season) in her spiritual journey. This is the very pinnacle of the Song of Solomon. She found a way to make it. Even though she had so many battles and struggles that she faced, she is now going to be seen as victorious as she arises from the wilderness. It is her Beloved who is asking a glorious question. It is a question of mystery and wonder. He says, "Who is this coming up from the wilderness, leaning upon her beloved?" How do we know that it was the Bride's Beloved asking this question? Because after He asked the question, He then says that He was the One who awakened her under the apple tree. Do you remember when we looked at the Shulamite sitting under the apple tree with great delight in Song of Solomon 2:3? It was the Beloved who awakened her in that strategic time. Now in Song of Solomon 8:5,

He is reminding her of where she had been and is declaring where she is now in her spiritual progress. He is basically letting her know that she is not the same person as before.

I believe it was the Bride's cry and her humble submission as a leaning Bride, that got her here to this place of victory. Her consistent cry to arise from the wilderness is what helped her reach her ultimate destination. She is victorious! She probably didn't fully understand the depth of what was being produced within her in the wilderness, but Jesus did. Let me ask you a question: do you really understand what your Beloved is producing in your heart in this season? Can you begin to see that you're not the same person anymore?

It is in the wilderness that Jesus is producing a deep cry of total dependence upon Him. He is producing a voice and the voice is what becomes our authority. John the Baptist was a voice crying out in the wilderness (see Matthew 3:3). His voice came from his cry. What was in him would come out. I believe that our authority comes from our voice and our voice comes from our cry. This is the beauty of our training while in the wilderness. We are being trained to lean through the desperate cry within.

Dependency: The Depth of Bridal Love

The Bride, just like Jacob in the Old Testament, has wrestled with God through her journey in the wilderness and is now limping and leaning upon Him. It was the Lord's strategy to produce in her an attitude of dependency upon Him. She is pictured as leaning in the Song of Solomon. She has learned to sit, to run, and to leap on mountains, but now she is doing something she has never done before. She has come to a place in her walk where it is no longer her strength carrying her, but it is His strength. She is leaning upon the One she loves and trusts. What a beautiful place she has entered into. Not only is she lovesick, but she is also leaning. She is giving herself in a new way compared to the last seven chapters, or seasons of her life.

The Bridal Seal of Fire

Dependency is one of the key purposes of our time spent in the wilderness. Many times we think that God is picking on us and making our lives difficult in the wilderness. We think He must be disappointed and frustrated with our constant failures, so He puts us in difficult circumstances and doesn't seem to really care about us anymore. Or we think that His patience has run out on us and now He's really going to give us what we deserve. But that is not the case with Jesus, the Bridegroom God. He is so far from those lies and accusations. He is actually working everything out for His ultimate pleasure and our ultimate good. It is in the wilderness that He is weakening our own strength and human zeal. He is not looking for strength and independence within us, but He is looking for leaning lovers whose weakness would be made perfect through His strength. That's His kind intention for us in the wilderness.

> *And He said to me, "My grace is sufficient for you, for My strength is made perfect in weakness." Therefore most gladly I will rather boast in my infirmities, that the power of Christ may rest upon me. Therefore I take pleasure in infirmities, in reproaches, in needs, in persecutions, in distresses, for Christ's sake. For when I am weak, then I am strong.*
> 2 Corinthians 12:9–10

There is a place of inner strength and protection that comes from living in the place of weakness, especially voluntary weakness. It's a choice of lifestyle. It is the place that you choose to make your Beloved the One who carries you through all the different seasons of your life. He is the One who becomes your only hope and way out of difficulty. He becomes the absolute source for every provision, small or big. Over the last few years, I have come to understand this reality about dependency and voluntary weakness: just when I think I have something to offer, I find I have nothing to offer; but when I realize that I have nothing to offer, I then have something to offer. The depth of bridal love is all about dependency.

The degree we cry and reach out for help from heaven is the degree of our dependency. Your cry reveals your dependency! A proud person doesn't think they really need help. But a humble person truly knows how much help they really need in their journey. May we learn to be those who would continually cry out and ask for help in all that we do, expressing our humility before God. There are two little words that I continually cry out to God, and are very powerful. They are the words "help me." I love to whisper this cry!

The Bride spent her entire journey in the wilderness, being trained within her heart to lean and to love. Now she is about to finish her race, her spiritual pilgrimage upon the earth. There are two key words mentioned in Song of Solomon 8:5: "up" and "from." She is being pictured coming up from the wilderness. The word "up" means that she is being carried by another Person and is ascending into greatness. She will no longer stay where she was. She is ascending up.

The word "from" means that she is coming out of one thing and is being brought into something new. In Song of Solomon 1, it was the King who escorted her into His chambers. She was brought into something. But now she is escorted up from the wilderness. She is coming out of it. Basically said, she is being exalted from the wilderness into Jesus Himself. He will become the seal upon her heart; that is where she is heading. She is not destined to stay in the wilderness the whole time, but is destined to come up from the wilderness.

I have really good news for you. You, as a Shulamite, who are in the process of becoming a leaning Bride have been destined by the heart of God to come up from the wilderness before you finish your spiritual journey in this age. It is His passion and strength and commitment working within you to complete you. Just as God brought the children of

The Bridal Seal of Fire

Israel out of Egypt and just as He brought the Bride out of the wilderness, so He will do the same for you. You are destined for greatness! You're destined to be revived again. You are destined to abide in Christ with a heart set ablaze. You will come up restored because you simply allow the Lord to carry you and you will not quit in the wilderness. Amen!

Let us again hear the testimony of David in Psalm 71 while he was in the wilderness facing intense suffering. In fact, he is the one who says that it was God who had made him see great and severe troubles; yet declared that He would deliver him out of them and would make him great.

> *You, who have shown me great and severe troubles, shall revive me again, and bring me up again from the depths of the earth. You shall increase my greatness, and comfort me on every side.*
>
> Psalm 71:20–21

Do you notice the words "up again?" David says that God would bring him up again from the depths of the earth. He is referring to the place of the wilderness. God delivered him before, and He will do it again in the present and future. David would not stay there in the place of severe troubles forever, but would be restored. That was his hope in the midst of the battle!

I believe this revelation that David received is very similar to the Bride coming up from the wilderness in Song of Solomon 8:5. She had seen great troubles and difficulties. She probably wondered how long it would be before she would find the place of victory. She probably wondered if she would ever come up from the wilderness. But she did. Hallelujah!

After Jesus asks the question, "Who is this coming up from the wilderness," He then immediately breaks out with a request of the Bride. It is actually His cry deep inside *His* heart. Over the last seven chapters, we have seen the Shulamite's cry being portrayed, but now we come to the ultimate cry and it's the cry of the Bridegroom God. I believe He was so moved by her distinct cries in her journey that now He can't take it anymore. Now it's His turn to reveal His deep longing and cry. We will soon discover that He longs for His Bride to give Him first place in her life. He wants to be the very flame and seal upon her heart.

All throughout the Song of Solomon, Jesus has been affirming the heart of the Shulamite who has now become a Bride. He has been calling her forth into her prophetic destiny. There are only two times in the Song of Solomon when He makes a request of her. The first request is found in Song of Solomon 2. He asked her to arise and ascend unto the mountains with Him. His second request is found in Song of Solomon 8. Now He is going to unveil His cry and let the one He loves so much know exactly what it is He desires and wants from her.

Understanding the Bridal Seal of Fire

Jesus, the Bridegroom, wastes no time in revealing what has been burning on His heart for such a long time. I am sure He wanted to ask this request earlier in the Shulamite's journey, but He knew that she was not ready. But now is the set time. She is more than ready. So what is His request? He asks her to set Him as a seal upon her own heart. That's His cry!

> *Set me as a seal upon your heart, as a seal upon your arm; for love is as strong as death, jealousy as cruel as the grave; its flames are flames of fire, a most vehement flame.*
>
> Song of Solomon 8:6

When Jesus requested her to go up to the mountains with Him, it was mostly for her sake. But now as He requests her to set Him as a seal upon her heart, it is mostly for His sake. This is His supreme cry and desire in the Song of Solomon.

The Bridal Seal of Fire

Yes, the whole focus of this book peers into the Shulamite's cry and I want to keep it as the focus, but I do want us to see that Jesus Himself has a cry for something as well.

The Bride does say yes to Jesus' loving request. She immediately responds to His supreme cry. She does set Him as a seal upon her heart. Her training in the wilderness prepared her for the divine seal. She learned a powerful lesson on her journey, and that lesson was not to delay in whatever her Beloved requested of her. She failed with Jesus' first request in Song of Solomon 2, but she passed the test in Song of Solomon 8. She now fully obeys and says yes to whatever He desires and requests from her. Remember, she fully belongs to Him now. She is walking the pathway of Lordship. She is in the relationship for Him completely. Maybe you're thinking to yourself, how do we know for sure that she said yes to Jesus' request? Let us see what she has to say at the very end of her spiritual journey.

> *But my own vineyard is mine to give; the thousand shekels are for you, O Solomon, and two hundred are for those who tend its fruit.*
> Song of Solomon 8:12, NIV

This is a bold and powerful testimony. She tells Jesus that her vineyard is for Him. Remember, the vineyard represents the garden of her heart. She is giving her whole life away to Him without any hesitation. Earlier, in Song of Solomon 1, she was too busy and was not tending the garden of her heart (1:6). But now, not only is she tending her garden, but she's giving it completely away to the One she loves. This confession came from the seal of fire abiding in her heart!

The bridal seal in Song of Solomon 8:6 that she said yes to has now become her authority. She didn't earn it, but she cried out and sought after it with all of her heart. She knows the great worth and value of this seal of fire.

Let us take a look at what this seal is and get a better

understanding of it. The Hebrew word for "seal" is *chowtham*. It means a seal or a signet ring. A seal or signet ring was the emblem of authority worn on the right hand (see Genesis 41:42). In the ancient world, kings put a "seal of wax" on important documents. They secured them with wax and then stamped the wax with the king's signet ring. The royal seal spoke of the king's ownership, protection, authority and guarantee that what was on the documents was backed up by all the power of his kingdom. If the royal seal was broken, it was a serious crime that led to the death penalty. If even a government official broke the royal seal without the king's permission, he would be put to death.

For us personally, the seal is not a seal of an earthly king, but it is the seal of the heavenly King. The seal is a living person. Jesus Himself is the source of the seal. To set Him as the seal upon our hearts means we are inviting His fiery love and passion to touch and seal our inner man. It's a vast statement of humility. It is a statement of giving God that which no one else can give Him—our love. That which He imparts will be given back to Him in complete, voluntary obedience. It is the divine exchange of love.

Jesus is the One who has complete authority and ownership over us because He redeemed us to the Father by His own blood. He is the One in whom we find divine protection in this dark age. He has sealed us by the power of the Holy Spirit, who guarantees our future inheritance.

> *In Him you also trusted, after you heard the word of truth, the gospel of your salvation; in whom also, having believed, you were sealed with the Holy Spirit of promise, who is the guarantee of our inheritance until the redemption of the purchased possession, to the praise of His glory.*
>
> Ephesians 1:13–14

I believe the bridal seal is mostly expressed in Isaiah 53.

The Bridal Seal of Fire

It reveals the death of the innocent One for the deliverance of the guilty one. It is the greatest chapter in the Bible on true greatness. The Cross is God's relentless passion and desire for humans. Isaiah the prophet says that Jesus was led like a Lamb to the slaughter, and that it greatly pleased the Father to bruise and crush Him (see Isaiah 53:7, 10). Not only was He led and crushed by the wrath of God, but He poured out His soul unto death (see Isaiah 53:12). That's the distinct mark of this bridal seal. Jesus held nothing back in His pursuit for the hearts of men. His soul was completely poured out, giving everything within His own being for the sake of love. His relentless passion for mankind is the seal itself.

Jesus' love, humility, meekness, submission, suffering, obedience and exaltation stand alone. There is absolutely no other human being who can compare or even come close to Him. Jesus proved and demonstrated His love that is strong as death at Golgotha. Nothing could stop the flame of love that was in His heart as He set His face like flint to Jerusalem. It is why He has the right to ask the request, "Set me as a seal upon your heart."

This seal reveals Jesus' passionate love, which is stronger than death. That is the strength of the bridal seal. It is a love that burns like blazing fire. It burns like a mighty flame. The Hebrew expression conveys the idea of a most intense flame. You can actually feel the tangible glow of this blaze of fire in your spirit. It's so powerful! This kind of love cannot be extinguished or drowned. It is the very "flame of Jehovah." He is the fire itself. He desires to impart His fire into the very core of our beings. He longs to set us ablaze like never before because He is an all–consuming fire.

For the Lord your God is a consuming fire, a jealous God.
Deuteronomy 4:24

God is a consuming fire! His whole being is set ablaze

with heat. Daniel the Prophet tells us that there is a river of fire flowing, coming out before Him (see Daniel 7:10). John the Apostle tells us that Jesus' eyes are like blazing fire (see Revelation 1:14). Ezekiel had an incredible revelation of the beauty and majesty of Jesus' fire. In Ezekiel 1, he sees a Man sitting upon a sapphire throne, consumed with fire from head to toe, and was surrounded by a brilliant light. He causes all angelic beings to tremble before him.

> *Above the expanse over their heads was what looked like a throne of sapphire, and high above on the throne was a figure like that of a man. I saw that from what appeared to be his waist up he looked like glowing metal, as if full of fire, and that from there down he looked like fire; and brilliant light surrounded him. Like the appearance of a rainbow in the clouds on a rainy day, so was the radiance around him. This was the appearance of the likeness of the glory of the Lord. When I saw it, I fell facedown, and I heard the voice of one speaking.*
> Ezekiel 1:26–28, NIV

There is nothing that can stop the all-consuming fire of God's being. It spreads and moves with such force. His fire penetrates everything that it comes in touch with. It is unquenchable. There is absolutely no opposition that can quench its heat. It can never be put out. When we come into contact with this bridal seal of fire, we do not remain the same anymore. His fire empowers and tenderizes our hearts to love God. It enables us to become wholehearted just like the Shulamite, who became the Bride of Christ. God's jealous love burns away all the things within us that are not everlasting and He purifies all that will remain forever.

Jesus' love is pictured as being strong as death. The word strong means powerful, irresistible, mighty and fierce. The jealousy of love is hard, cruel, and firm as Sheol. Jealousy here is simply asserting the right of possession or ownership, just as Sheol takes full possession of the dead (see

Psalm 49:13–15). Death is the strongest and final enemy to be destroyed. It claims everything in the natural realm and is never satisfied. It is very cruel and never feels sorry for anyone. The energy of God's love is compared to the energy of death and Sheol. It is unyielding as the grave. That is how powerful and unmoving Jesus' love is.

The Power of the Bridal Seal

Many waters cannot quench love, nor can the floods drown it. If a man would give for love all the wealth of his house, it would be utterly despised.
Song of Solomon 8:7

The love of Jesus is unstoppable. Nothing will ever overpower His love. Not even many waters can put out the fire of His love. Many waters is a powerful imagery for threatening forces, opposition or difficult circumstances. The enemy will send the waters of disappointment, temptation, hopelessness, loneliness, depression, grief, pain and persecution to try and put out the fire of God in our lives. He will tell you that life is not fair or God is not fair. He will tell you that your present situation will never end, or you're the only one who is really going through this difficult time. But we must not allow the enemy to try and drown us with the waters and floods of life. We must surrender and yield to Jesus' passionate love for us, so that any storm that tries to take us out will come crashing down and will melt before our own very eyes. No matter how great the addiction or severe trauma, no matter how painful your marriage, no matter how difficult your life, there is nothing that can challenge or conquer the fire of God when yielded to. It's indestructible!

Water always puts out fire in the natural realm. It's like the law of gravity–it's going to happen every single time. But the fire of God is supernatural. It can never be put out. It is far above the law of gravity. If the Bride received this fire that would never go out in her journey, then surely it will happen to us as we say yes to His outrageous love!

In Exodus 3, we have a great picture of God's fire as He appears to Moses from the midst of a burning bush. What was God trying to teach Moses through the burning bush?

He was revealing Himself as the God of burning passion and the God of tender compassion towards the children of Israel. The unquenchable fire was a prophetic sign of how He felt in His heart towards them. In Exodus 2, the children of Israel were in bondage under Pharaoh's leadership and were being harshly treated and persecuted. So they began to cry out to the Lord for help. Their cry came up to God because of the bondage they were in. God heard their cry! He remembered His covenant that He made with Abraham, Isaac and Jacob, and He looked upon them with tender mercy. So what does God do about the condition of His chosen people? He appeared to Moses in the midst of a burning bush. God wanted Moses to fully understand His fiery commitment and passion for those who belong to Him.

How God felt towards His people is what He imparted to Moses. Not only did God want to reveal what His heart was like to Moses, but He also wanted to make him become a deliverer of the nation of Israel. God was not content for just Moses to understand His burning passion. He was going to use him in a very strategic way to deliver the nation of Israel from bondage. So that is why He appeared to him in a burning bush. Moses was being trained to deliver God's people through the revelation of God's supernatural fire that would never go out.

If God can hear the cry of the children of Israel while in bondage, He can hear the cry of His Shulamite's while in bondage. He will appear to us as the God of supernatural fire. He will appear to us and equip us to become delivers of those who are under bondage. There is no flood of sin or failure that can drown Jesus' strong love for us. In the midst of persecution, temptation and even martyrdom, the heart that is sealed with fiery love will not be moved, shaken or separated. Paul

The Bridal Seal of Fire

the Apostle received this revelation in his life.

> *Who shall separate us from the love of Christ? Shall tribulation, or distress, or persecution, or famine, or nakedness, or peril, or sword? As it is written: For Your sake we are killed all day long; we are accounted as sheep for the slaughter. Yet in all these things we are more than conquerors through Him who loved us. For I am persuaded that neither death nor life, nor angels nor principalities nor powers, nor things present nor things to come, nor height nor depth, nor any other created thing, shall be able to separate us from the love of God which is in Christ Jesus our Lord.*
> Romans 8:35–39

Not only is the bridal seal as strong as death and unyielding as the grave, not only does it burn like blazing fire and like a mighty flame, not only is it unquenchable from the waters and rivers of life, but it is pictured as being priceless. Jesus validates this as He declares, "If a man would give for love all the wealth of his house, it would be utterly despised" (see Song of Solomon 8:7). That is the power and outworking of the bridal seal. This love in God's heart cannot be bought or purchased with money, and any attempt to buy it would be utterly scorned. It is irreplaceable!

As the Bride receives the seal upon her heart, she is now fully obeying Jesus without any regard to cost. There were probably some times on her journey when she obeyed because she had to, and there might have been times when she thought she was paying the price to love Jesus with all of her heart. But now she is a voluntary lover who has no price tags. She doesn't recognize sacrifice. It is a profound joy and delight. There are no pockets of resistance within her. She is a woman who's consumed with burning love and is shining just like her Beloved. Her power to love Jesus is her reward.

People without the revelation of Jesus' blazing love for them are the ones who will count the cost. They seem to serve out of duty rather than delight. If paying the price is a major struggle for you, than ponder upon this reality: Jesus was fully God, yet laid aside the garments of deity, and took upon Himself the garments of humanity. He stepped into the earth and was crushed by the wrath of His own Father just for us. Then you and I continually resisted Him, but He kept on pursuing us and chasing us down. He totally forgave us freely and made us kings and priests in His kingdom for eternity. We didn't want Him but He wanted us. We didn't deserve to be crowned as a Bride, but He made us fully clean and deserving to receive the crown of glory! Hopefully, this will help change our attitude and perspective about paying the price.

> *And when the Chief Shepherd appears, you will receive the crown of glory that does not fade away.*
>
> 1 Peter 5:4

I believe when we, as Shulamite's, remember Calvary and stare into the eyes of the wounded Man in heaven, then whatever sacrifice and struggle we face will not even compare to what we have in Him. He is far worth more than any sacrifice. When our eyes gaze upon the slain Lamb who was wounded for love, then paying the price will not even come into the picture. Listen to what Paul has to say from his own personal experience about this.

> *But what things were gain to me, these I have counted loss for Christ. Yet indeed I also count all things loss for the excellence of the knowledge of Christ Jesus my Lord, for whom I have suffered the loss of all things, and count them as rubbish, that I may gain Christ and be found in Him, not having my own righteousness, which is from the law, but that which is through faith in Christ, the righteousness which is from God by faith; that I may know Him and the power of His resurrection, and the fellowship of His sufferings, being conformed to His death.*
>
> Philippians 3:7–10

The Bridal Seal of Fire

Four Aspects of the Bridal Seal

1. It imparts the glory of Jesus' love in our hearts. It is what empowers and tenderizes us to love God more. When we experience this glory of fire, it is where the heart begins to take off and soar like an eagle. It is exhilarating and fascinating. There is no greater feeling.
2. It burns away all the dross and purges all that gets in its way in our lives. This can become very painful at times, but it is necessary so we can become a prepared Bride for the last day (see Malachi 3:2–3).
3. It delivers God's people who are in bondage from the oppressors like in Exodus 2. It is the mark of protection, just like we see in the 144,000 Jewish believers in Revelation 7. The seal is the mark of the call of God upon a person's life and ministry.
4. It will utterly destroy the enemies of the worthy Lamb of God. His fire will consume them.

The bridal seal of fire is powerful! It is a mighty weapon coming from the very throne of God. It is the relentless fulfillment of the kiss of God upon the human heart (see Song of Solomon 1:2). It is the completion of our journey to wholehearted love. It is the seal that completes us in the grace of God. It is where we are heading in our future. To have this supernatural fire abiding in our heats doesn't come overnight. Just as it took the Shulamite eight chapters to get this seal of fire and become the Bride, so it will take time for us to get it as well. There will be a struggle and a wrestling during our pursuit. There is no true victory without a fight. But the good news is this: the Father in heaven will not relent until He has a Bride burning with the seal of His Son's own fire. He wants us to love Him as He loves us. The Father has promised to give Jesus an eternal companion as His inheritance—a Bride who voluntarily chooses to be equally yoked with Him in love. This will be the beauty and glory of Jesus' wedding day. It is the great prize of all ages that He awaits.

Redemption finds its consummation in a Hallelujah chorus, a wedding feast, and a Bride dressed in white. It is the consummation at the marriage of the Lamb. In Revelation 19, we see the literal end of our journey in this age and the beginning of the next. It is the greatest picture of what true love is all about. You cannot have any higher price than God giving Himself for love.

> *Then I heard what sounded like a great multitude, like the roar of rushing waters and like loud peals of thunder, shouting: "Hallelujah! For our Lord God Almighty reigns. Let us be glad and rejoice and give Him glory, for the marriage of the Lamb has come, and His wife has made herself ready." And to her it was granted to be arrayed in fine linen, clean and bright, for the fine linen is the righteous acts of the saints.*
>
> Revelation 19:6–8, NIV

The Bridal Seal: The Marriage of the Lamb

The Bible has one grand theme running through the pages–a wedding! Jesus' public ministry began at a wedding (see John 2), and His public return will end with a wedding (see Revelation 19). This wedding, in the heart and mind of God, has been the blueprint from which the Godhead has been operating from since the very beginning of time. The marriage of the Lamb is one of the greatest events that will take place in the age to come. It is so glorious!

Do you fully understand where you are heading in your future destiny? Do you realize what is going to take place when you die? You are going to be married to Jesus, the Bridegroom God. It's why He died for you and pursued you. He is very determined to have a bridal partner right at His side forever. Being married to Jesus is not a physical union with Him, but it's a union of spirit.

The Bridal Seal of Fire

But he who is joined to the Lord is one spirit with Him.
1 Corinthians 6:17

Let us look in more detail at some of the history behind a wedding in the Bible in order to better understand the marriage of the Lamb. Weddings in Israel took place before the local town elders rather than before the priests (see Ruth 4:10–11). They transpired in homes rather than in the tabernacle or temple. The marriage was centered on two events: the Betrothal and the Wedding. The Jewish terms for the two events are Kiddushin and Chuppah. Here are five steps that took place in ancient Jewish marriage.

1. *The betrothal*: It was the time when the arrangement for the marriage was contracted. The groom's parents selected a bride for their son. This involved securing permission of the bride's parents and approval of both the bride and the groom themselves. The dates for the betrothal and wedding ceremonies were chosen and fixed. On the day of the betrothal, the engaged couple drank from the same cup, over which the betrothal benediction was pronounced, and then they took an oath to seal their betrothal to each other. This vow was ceremoniously repeated on the day of the wedding. The betrothal was equally as binding as the marriage itself.

2. *The wedding procession*: It was accomplished when the groom went to the house of the bride to fetch her to his home, and he went out to meet her. He was accompanied by a group of close friends. When the bridegroom arrived at the bride's house, he had to pay a purchase price in order to establish the marriage covenant. Young Jewish men had to buy their wives in Bible times.

3. *The wedding ceremony*: It was the time when the two of them were recognized as husband and wife in a legal sense.

4. *The wedding feast or banquet:* It followed the wedding ceremony. The couple feasted with their friends, usually for seven days following the wedding ceremony. It was a time of great enjoyment and celebration.
5. *The wedding night:* The married couple became one in flesh through their first sexual union. It was a night of romance and great joy.

The End of Our Journey

Just as weddings have taken place all throughout Church history, so there will be an ultimate wedding, the marriage of the Lamb. It will be the culmination of the ages. What a grand day it will be! The Song of Solomon calls the marriage of the Lamb the day of the gladness of Jesus' heart.

> *Go forth, O daughters of Zion, and see King Solomon with the crown with which his mother crowned him on the day of his wedding, the day of the gladness of his heart.*
> Song of Solomon 3:11

It is Jesus' day! Besides the Cross and the Resurrection, I believe that Jesus' wedding day will be the greatest and happiest day for Him. He has waited so long for this glorious time. He looks forward to it with such excitement. He will be the One wearing the crown. It is a wedding crown. Just as kings would wear their crown after conquering a nation, so He will wear His crown, as He conquers the hearts of His people for Himself. We will join the hosts of angels, saying, "worthy is the Lamb!"

Jesus is coming soon to make you His eternal companion. He will have an equally–yoked Bride, sealed and marked for His wedding day. You will be His forever because He fought for you. Somebody believed in you and did something about it. Somebody pursued you. Somebody fought for your freedom. Someone is coming to get you! Someone is preparing a gorgeous, gigantic city for you (see Hebrews 11:16). Jesus,

The Bridal Seal of Fire

the slain Lamb, paid a great price so you can be invited to the marriage of the Lamb. The path of Jesus was marked with wounds and the future destiny of His Bride is marked with glory. Hallelujah!

The Bride on the last day is soaring and rejoicing with a glad heart because she sees the wisdom of how God led her through the wilderness, just like the Bride in Song of Solomon 8:5. She will have clear understanding of how all of her circumstances were divinely arranged by the King Himself. It is part of the preparation for the wedding. When the end–time Bride of Christ stands upon the sea of glass like crystal, everything will all make sense before God's glorious throne.

God the Father is so determined to see that you are fully prepared for the wedding day of His own Son. He not only wants you there, but He wants you prepared. Maybe some of you are always wondering why you are going through such struggles and difficulties. You wonder why all the pain and suffering in your life. The reason is not because God is mad at you or is picking on you, but He's doing what is right and best for you. He doesn't want you coming up short in any area of your life. Would you just take a moment right now and personally thank Him.

It is so important that we are found prepared for this glorious day. Are you actually preparing for the great wedding of the Bridegroom King? What are some practical things that you are doing to have your heart equipped and prepared to meet Jesus face to face? Think about it and then take some time to wait upon the Lord and let Him shine His light upon you and let you know.

We must not only be prepared but informed about this glorious event. So many believers have no clue about their future destiny and inheritance. It is very important for us to know what is going to happen. It is our journey that we are discovering! Let us take a look at *five simple observations* concerning the marriage of the Lamb.

First: *A wedding will take place.* This is the final consummation in history. It is the completion of the betrothal. We have been invited to the most profound wedding celebration. This is what our lives are all about on the earth. The bridal feast is the highest calling in the eyes of God. Not even the angels have this privilege, but they have the desire to look into it (see 1 Peter 1:12). The Father has arranged a marriage for His Son (see Matthew 22:2). The Greek word for marriage in Revelation 19:7 is *gamos*. It speaks of an intimate union of fellowship. It is very personal.

Second: *We will be married to the Lamb.* It doesn't say that we will be married to the Judge, married to the King or married to the Almighty, but we will be married to the Lamb. Why the Lamb? Because He was slain (bears the marks of slaughter) and was the only One worthy to open the scroll in Revelation 5. Even when He had all the glory, He gladly laid it all down for the sake of love. He deserves the reward of His suffering.

Third: *The Bride will be prepared at the end of the age.* This is the great work and commitment of the beautiful God, and it's the cry and willingness of the Bride. Together they are in complete harmony. The Bride will have said yes to everything that God was saying and doing. She does not enter into this engagement with reluctance. For the primary currency in eternity is voluntary love that has been formed in our hearts while upon the earth. It will not be the size of our ministries or the wisdom of our leadership, but it will be the size of our heart. And that's what really matters to God. When the Bride crowns the worthy Lamb of God, she will already have been fully prepared.

Fourth: *The Bride will be dressed in fine linen.* It was granted to her to be arrayed in fine linen (see Revelation 7:14). The linen has been washed white in the blood of the Lamb. A Bride in a white gown is pictured as a clean and pure lady who is ready to be presented to the man she loves on her wedding day. This is also the wedding garment spoken of in

The Bridal Seal of Fire

Matthew 22:12. Nobody has the right to attend the wedding if they are not wearing this garment washed with the blood of Jesus.

Fifth: *This will be the Bride's greatest day.* She is pictured with a heart full of gladness and rejoicing (see Revelation 19:7). On the last day, the Bride will have fully understood Jesus' leadership throughout history. His perfect leadership will have produced a Bride who says with joy, "Let us be glad and rejoice and give Him glory for the marriage of the Lamb has come, and His wife has made herself ready." The Bride is exceedingly happy when all the information is laid out and she sees that God strategically arranged circumstances, seasons and events to fully prepare her.

May you get excited! May your heart rejoice and become glad. May you cast the vision to the nations of the earth concerning the marriage of the Lamb, the bridal seal of fire. There is going to be a wedding! It is time to say yes right now and set Jesus as the seal upon your heart. It's time to cry out and go after the flame of love that burns deep in the heart of God. Once again, let's read the verse and make this a primary focus in our lives.

> *Set me as a seal upon your heart, as a seal upon your arm; for love is as strong as death, jealousy as cruel as the grave; its flames are flames of fire, a most vehement flame. Many waters cannot quench love, nor can the floods drown it. If a man would give for love all the wealth of his house, it would be utterly despised.*
> Song of Solomon 8:6–7

Remember, this is your journey that you are discovering in the Song of Solomon. It is your cry that will transform you from a Shulamite into a Bride. Hallelujah!

APPENDIX

Song of Solomon Resources

The Song of Songs is Mike Bickle's most popular teaching series. Mike has devoted twenty years of prayerful study and research covering each line of this divine love song. During the winter of 2007 he taught this completely revised and updated 24–part course. Packed with new material and fresh insight, this is his most comprehensive and powerful presentation to date.

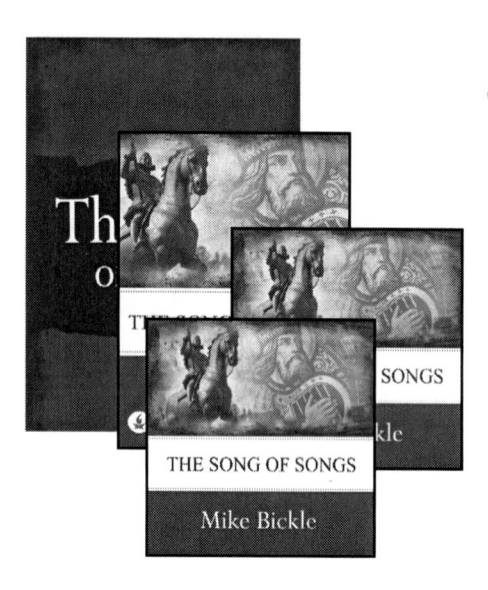

Song of Solomon Study Course

CD Set – $50
DVD Set – $75
MP3 Set – $25
Notes – $10

For more information and to order, go to www.IHOP.org.

Other Products by Mike Brumback

"HARP & BOWL" CDS

Throne of God 1 – Anointed CD that focuses on the beauty and majesty of God the Father and the throne room of heaven. It is combined with music, prophetic singing and inspirational prayers by Mike Brumback. Both singers, Julie Meyer and Paula Bowers, flow well, as they sing about the Jasper God in Revelation 4.

Throne of God 2 – A wonderful CD that has both beautiful worship songs and "harp & bowl" praying and singing. There are many great worship leaders from the International House of Prayer of Kansas City that are on it.

INSTRUMENTAL CD

Majesty – This is a fiery CD that has a strong sense and feel of the majesty that takes place in heaven. It is great for soaking, healing and deliverance. It is also great background music for your reading, studying and encountering time with Jesus.

STUDY GUIDE

Encountering the Throne of God
This is a verse by verse study of Revelation 4. It unveils the glory and majesty of the throne room of heaven. It develops the three distinct diamonds (jasper, sardius, emerald) that reflects who God the Father is. You will be absolutely fascinated and will marvel at the greatness and beauty of God's heart and His glorious throne.

BOOK

The Beauty of the Cross
Take another look at the heart of the Father over His Son from eternity past. It's a story of passion, determination and mercy for broken, sinful mankind. Jesus is a real person with real feelings and real struggles who fully identifies with us. He faced overwhelming pain, rejection, betrayal, abandonment, loneliness, and misunderstanding. As we peer into the bloody crucifixion, we discover the story of a triumphant, conquering King who is preparing His Bride to reign with Him forever.

Ordering Information

Mike Brumback
10981 College Lane
Kansas City, MO 64137
mikebrumback@ihop.org

These items can also be ordered from the International House of Prayer of Kansas City at www.IHOP.org.

Recommended Resources by Bob Sorge

These resources and more can be found at www.oasishouse.net.

In **SECRETS OF THE SECRET PLACE** Bob shares some of the secrets he's learned in making the secret place energizing and delightful. This has become Bob's bestseller. Gain fresh fuel for your secret devotional life with God!

This **COMPANION STUDY GUIDE**, when used with the Secrets book, comprises an unparalleled curriculum for igniting believers in the exhilarating delight of sitting at Jesus' feet and hearing His word. Designed for individual and small group usage.

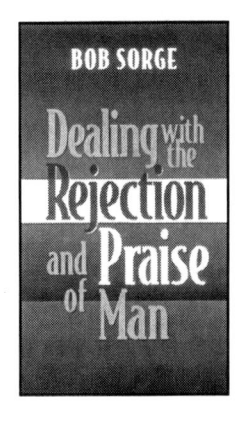

DEALING WITH THE REJECTION AND PRAISE OF MAN is a booklet that shows how to hold your heart before God in a way that pleases Him in the midst of both rejection and praise from people. Powerfully important reading for Christian leaders.

UNRELENTING PRAYER: Based upon the Luke 18 parable of the persistent widow, this book will increase your faith to remain fervent in prayer until God grants you justice from your adversary. Take a tender look at the issues of depression, reproach, and why God sometimes waits so long to answer our prayers. Your heart will be strengthened as you consider the restoration and restitution God intends to manifest in your life.

THE FIRE OF DELAYED ANSWERS explores how God sometimes delays the answers to our prayers in order to produce godly character in us. This book is "spiritual food" for those in crisis or difficulty.

PAIN, PERPLEXITY & PROMOTION looks at the book of Job from a fresh, prophetic vantage. Job's life shows how God promotes His chosen vessels to higher heights than they would have conceived possible. You won't find a more stirring, heart-felt book on Job.